Pearl Escapes

Fear of Success

By Pearl Howie

Author photo by Reinaldo Medina

Published by Pearl Escapes

www.pearlescapes.co.uk

pearl@pearlescapes.co.uk

Distributed in the UK by

Flying Machine Films Ltd.

Chichester Enterprise Centre, Terminus Rd, Chichester

West Sussex, PO19 8TX, United Kingdom

For my family

"A very Merry Christmas,
And a happy New Year,
Let's hope it's a good one,
Without any fear"
Happy Xmas (War Is Over), John Lennon & Yoko Ono
featuring Plastic Ono Band and Harlem Community Choir,
December 1971

Contents

Disclaimer

Trying to describe feelings and many of the concepts in this book with words is like trying to describe colours; if you understand what I mean by the word "blue" great, this will work for you, if not, if you imagine a darker colour, a lighter one, or a colour you would call "blue" but I would call "green", I am sorry that we are not able to connect, to communicate right now. Try again later.

I am only responsible for what I say, not for what you hear.

Foreword

Normally the foreword to a book is written by someone other than the author. The thing is that I am not the person who wrote this book, that person is gone. When I began writing this book I was a person in search of a book on fear of success, I was a person who could not write a book on fear of success because I did not understand fear of success - I thought I did not know enough. But as I started and took the first steps I realised that I had been practising and mastering escaping from the fear of success for years. I followed the yellow brick road and found the thing I sought was inside me all along.

Sometimes we say about people that they have been "working in the dark" but in a way I was "working in the light". Although I was facing my own fear of success (and still am) I was bringing that darkness into the light by doing what I called "feeling alive", by finding escapes – the most wonderful ways of healing and experiences around the world.

By the time I finish writing this book I will be a person capable of writing a book about fear of success, but I was already a person who had written many books on the subject – just under different names, different titles. Like many scientists who think they are trying to solve one problem, one illness, but end up solving something entirely different.

When I started teaching Zumba® Fitness I thought it was what I would do until I figured out what I was really doing – I didn't understand that it would teach me everything I needed for the next stage of my life – but that I would also have to let it go in order to continue.

When I started dancing salsa I was unable to dance salsa, but every second I got closer to being the person who could dance salsa.

But… (and I will talk much more about humility later) as the sages say, "It is better to know and think you do not know, than to not know and think that you do know." Or, another way of looking at it, is to remember that the painter who thinks he has mastered all forms of art is finished. In order to keep being a master of what we do, we have to remember that we are never finished; if we cannot learn something new, we must create something new.

Success is not static. Perhaps this thing we call achievement is. To have created, to have succeeded, is a wonderful thing. I feel immensely proud of the books I have written, but that work still needs to be cared for, built upon. (It's not as bad as gardening, but there is always work to be done on a book catalogue.) And I know that some of you, who are struggling with your first or second book, will hear the words "book catalogue" and breathe a little harder – it seems like a distant dream. Yes, but like a music single, then an album, then another, once we get into flow it's extraordinary what we can accomplish. I am a penniless writer, it is clear that I cannot rest on my laurels, but even if I could, even if I was a billionaire author, even when I had "bank," something drove me on. Perhaps one of our biggest fears of success is "What next?" "If I achieve this, if I do what I dream, if it becomes a reality, what will I do without that dream?"

So a word to ease the simple fear of success of an explorer (and we are all explorers), "There is always more to discover, more to explore, more to experience… there is always something amazing around the corner… never, ever, ever give up."

Introduction

Over and over again in the last few years I've realised what my problem is. Fear of success.

When I discovered, at the Jericho Writers' Festival of Writing in York that I was on the right track with my book series "Camino de la Luna," I felt terrible and had to go to bed early (leaving a formal dinner with top authors and agents), followed by several days of "freaking out" and riding out a wave of symptoms similar to PTSD.

What saved me at the time was sitting in a session the next day with the editor and author Debi Alper who was talking about facing our fears. She asked us what our fears were.

I felt so awful that I had nothing to lose, even though I was sure the rest of the group would hate me. I put my hand up, "Fear of success."

"Ah yes," she said, and proceeded to ask the authors in the room who had been signed by major agents and publishers what it had felt like for them.

Suddenly the room was full of people nodding, yes, this thing we were all there for, this getting published, this Holy Grail, all of it, was something we were pursuing, at the same time as not having a clue how to handle it if we did catch it (a lot like a dog chasing a cat, really).

At the time I didn't Google it or try to find books about it, I was too busy riding it out.

Day by day I took another brave step in the direction I had set out to follow. I learned how to check my books' positions on the Amazon charts. I went to the first book and looked down. It was a freebie version of "Camino de la Luna – Take What You Need" and it was at position 115 or thereabouts in the Travel chart. Oh my gosh, I had expected it would take ages to move on up, but I was almost, almost visible.

In my book "free Feeling Real Emotions Everyday" I wrote a beautiful piece which goes, "This is not fear, this is excitement..." and I've used it many times to help me get through barriers and challenges. But no matter how many times I told myself, I was still having to work really hard to hold it together.

It went into the charts. I remember I was in a Premier Inn, working on uploading other versions of the books, surrounded by fluffy pillows in a deep, soft bed. It was a cushion I needed as I drank a dozen cups of tea, but I wasn't celebrating, I was withstanding the success, the feeling of being on show, of placing, of arriving.

Over the last year I have hit Amazon Best Seller status in 26 paid categories, I kind of enjoy it now. I don't know how many times I've hit the Best Seller status in the Free charts (although my latest book did just hit no. 20-25 in the US and UK Kindle charts for Legal Thrillers and Financial Thrillers. Which was nice.) Almost every time it's got easier. I've realised that the sky isn't going to fall in, I'm not going to be hounded by journalists, and sadly, I'm not going to be a billionaire any time soon. Sometimes it has made me so happy, other times incredulous, other times deeply moved and sad that the person who inspired me wasn't with me, but I enjoy it now. I don't freak out, I don't hide in bed, sometimes I do have to go for a walk along the beach, but most of the time I just feel honoured, and privileged, like when one of my books finally hit the Meditation chart and I felt like I was in a select group of people who I deeply admire, people like Thich Nhat Hanh and Pema Chödrön.

All it took was a bit of practice.

But over the last year, and actually more than a decade ago, I have Googled "fear of success," I have done quizzes and questionnaires, I have watched YouTube videos, I have researched "Imposter Syndrome", and yet nowhere have I found a definitive answer to the question, "What is fear of success?" and perhaps more importantly, "What can we do about it, short of just pushing through in the haphazard way I have been doing?"

I have found people saying such unhelpful things as, "There's no such thing as fear of success, just fear of hard work." In my experience that's just not true.

When I wrote my book "Meditation for Angry People," it was easy. I had been thinking about and practising these meditations for years, they were at my fingertips, yet fear of success is something different, it seems to vanish like smoke every time I feel I am closing in on it. Like the secret in "Buffy the Vampire Slayer" that Glory is Ben, it seems to be a mystical secret that defies conscious consistency, that, like a state of enlightenment, we lose as soon as we grasp it.

I'm a mystic.

I fight fear.

I'm going in.

How to Use This Book

A good way to use a spiritual or mystical book is to open it at random. Or you could read it from the start to finish, or from the back to the front. Your answers will find you as long as you are open to and ready for them.

This book is structured in three main parts:-

1. The problem

2. Solutions

3. Origins of the problem

In my experience, if we spend too long looking at the problem it can be hard to see solutions, so I have tried to get us from the problem to the solution as quickly as possible – this should work for many types of fear of success. However, sometimes we need to look into the cause, the reason, the deep underlying roots of where our thinking got twisted around, where we learned to be so afraid. But please don't dwell here. Get in, get what you need and get out again. You are not meant to live here, just to visit and understand. Don Miguel Ruiz says that we are addicted to our suffering, so when we look into the darkness do so with care, and then step back out into the light. Do not hulk this stuff around with you, "Oh I'm so fearful of success because my parents treated me this way or that way…" remember, they did their best and without them you would not be here right now. Show a little respect and honour where you come from.   (It's one of the Ten Commandments.)

The

Problem

What Is Fear of Success?

I think there are a number of types of fear of success.

1. Fear of false success

What do I mean by this? I mean the icky fear of actually achieving what other people define as success. It's a classic reason for people "failing" – because the dream was never theirs in the first place. What if your parents want you to become a lawyer or a doctor, or a pop star, but it gives you night sweats? Is it because this is a trap, a place you do not want to be? Many people may feel they have a fear of success, or a fear of hard work, but the real fear is that, given the path they are on, if they keep on going, they might just end up where they are headed.

2. Fear of consequences of success

This is another popular theory I discovered on the internet. The fear of responsibility, riches, envy, standing out from the crowd, exposure. The fear of losing one's free time. The fear of having to do things we don't like as part of our success. "Year of Yes" by Shonda Rhimes is a fascinating account of her experience of hiding from success, or rather all the parts of success she told herself she wasn't comfortable with, instead of owning it.

3. *Fear of being, doing, having the very thing we want*

(Austin Powers wants me to say, "This is me in a nutshell.")

We want to dive off the high board, but it terrifies us. We want to afford a luxury massage, but we make excuses why not. We want the contract to write a red hot novel, but the thought of sitting down and writing the words on a page makes us find a million displacement activities. If success is just doing the thing, regardless of critical or financial success, why does sitting down to write create such existential crises that writers are known as possibly the worst group of drunks, sexaholics, morphine addicts and suicidal freaks amongst all the self-destructive arty farty types? Why do I personally need to remind myself constantly to stay off the drugs, and to drink what I nickname "The Hemingway" - a virgin mohito or lemonade, until I've actually finished writing for the day? Is this the heart of Marianne Williamson's "our greatest fear is not that we are inadequate, it is that we are powerful beyond measure"? Perhaps.

Eleanor Roosevelt said a thing. It was, "You must do the thing you think you cannot do." In my experience I've found it, more often than not, to be the way forward.

In my own words, my ego says, "I can't do this, I can't do this, I can't do this."

And I say, in reply (as Joey once almost said in "Friends"), "Do it anyway."

(Or more recently I like the phrase, "Actually, I can.")

Or sometimes I just say, "Shush." (Which reminds me, I have quite a few videos on YouTube explaining these techniques.)

And sometimes I pretend I'm Elmer Fudd and I say to my ego, "Be very qwuiet, I'm hunting wabbits."

4. Fear of loss of success

When I first heard this (it was the first video on YouTube for fear of success) I thought this was fear of failure dressed up as fear of success, but the more I thought about it, the more I realised that there is a great deal to understand about this fear. For example, we fear getting into relationships and succeeding because we may one day lose the relationship.

Every second we stay in the relationship feels as though disaster is getting closer, each step we take into what we want we become more vulnerable. For those of us who have experienced a fear of commitment or intimacy it's frightening and disturbing that what should be wonderful moments of romance and joy feel like death, and, if we are aware, bring up feelings of terror.

It feels like staying in a game of poker, where with each date, each kiss, the stakes get higher. And the risk of falling feels unimaginable, and yet the risk of staying in the game feels too much. It feels like deciding when to jump off a moving train.

A bereaved mother once said a beautiful thing about the short time she had with her daughter, who was born with a terminal and acute illness, "There is only one choice, the choice between pain and regret."

And yet, looking back on my romantic relationships, I understand things on a different level, that that fear and that choice to take the path of regret in relationships, to run away or to sabotage, was born of something else.

For many of us, we have already experienced loss. We just haven't allowed ourselves to fully feel the pain.

For many of us, that choice wasn't really a choice. We loved openly and without question, perhaps a friend, perhaps a brother, perhaps a parent or another family member, maybe even a birth parent that we didn't consciously remember, and then in a natural and ferocious way, we lost them.

And we did what we had to do to survive, what we humans do; we went into denial. We went into a space of saying, "I don't care." We started a lie, we started to practice black magic upon ourselves – what we can call it when we use our words against ourselves. "I'm okay." "It doesn't matter." "I never knew my dad, and you can't miss what you never had."

Falling in love makes us vulnerable. Not just to the possibility of hurt, rejection, loss in the future, but it makes us more vulnerable to uncovering the lie at the heart of our lives (because these are important lies, not "I missed the bus and that's why I'm late").

In the fairy tale, Sleeping Beauty is awoken by true love's kiss (and don't all spells end the same way?) True love, unconditional love ends all curses. Didn't you know that?

But waking up is painful, awareness can be excruciating, which is why we avoid becoming who we truly are – why we avoid success, our feelings, our true nature, because if I stay asleep, drunk, high, workaholic, perfectionist, OCD, even high on spiritual vibes, I get to pretend that I'm okay a little bit longer.

The bereaved mother was right, "There is one choice, pain or regret." But this choice is slightly different, because we already had the blow that caused the pain, so our choice is to stay in limbo, in that moment between cause and effect, in that moment, in that space, which is no space at all, which is claustrophobic and suffocating, a freeze frame, a fragment of life, afraid to move forward into the future, afraid of the light, afraid to experience heaven because we know a part of it is going to feel like hell. We stay in a space where there is no room to grow, because any bigger and we shatter illusions, break through the box we have built around ourselves and then we will have no choice but to live our lives.

The regret, the regret is what we experience when we turn around when it is too late and see that we, in the words of "Strictly Ballroom," "lived our lives in fear." That we were too scared to truly live.

This fear also masquerades as illusions, or fake fears:-

Fear of being a has-been

What if I do this and it's the best I can ever do? What if I shoot for the moon and I fall, I fail. Shouldn't I wait for a better opportunity?

You have to trust your heart, but I would say, if it is not the right time, well, the universe has a way of making sure you catch the right train, and sometimes it is only in catching the wrong train that we get experience, that we practice.

The more you reach, and try, the better you will get at recognising what is right for you.

And sometimes we have to do our absolute best in one field of endeavour in order to let that go and move onto something new. Perhaps it is the best we can do, but there is also peace in reaching our limits in one area of our life and feeling free to walk away. "I've reached the top and had to stop and that's what's bothering me..." King Louie, from "The Jungle Book".

Do not be afraid of hitting the glass ceiling, Charlie did it, in "Charlie and the Chocolate Factory".

Fear of making mistakes

You get the job, or the interview, or the date. You're terrified you're going to do something wrong. Don't worry. You will. There is no way forward without tripping and falling. Do your best and forgive yourself for needing practice. Embrace your mistakes, be honest and apologise and learn from them. Do your best to learn from other people's mistakes, it's cheaper. Do it anyway. Take a breath, slow down, don't let your ego freak you out, use the Force, and you will make mistakes, you will have AFGO moments (Another F%$ing Growth Opportunity) but you will probably have less than if you lose focus or try to bluster through. (When I am very tired and travelling I remind myself – this is the moment when I have to be slow and careful – and somehow I don't leave my glasses in the hotel shower. Often.)

5. *Fear of what we falsely believe we need to do, to be, have in order to be successful*

I'm going to come back to this in some of the other chapters (take a look in the Contents if there's something you specifically want answered), and this is very close to fear of false success, but this one, this one is extremely pervasive and damaging, and can even set in long after you are already successful, and so I really want to examine it properly.

I've read a lot of business books, self-help books, what I'd call success books, and many of them are not afraid of giving out rules. There also hosts of social media influencers and sports people who will make big, bold statements about how they achieved success, and even the perfume ads and the sports drinks slogans telling you how to live your life.

If this is ringing lots of bells for you I highly recommend you read "The Four Agreements" and then "The Fifth Agreement" (which is "Be sceptical, but learn to listen"). I am the annoying person who sits there at business events disagreeing with everyone. One of the major problems is language. (Again, "The Four Agreements" and Derrida are very useful, as is Shakespeare, "What's in a name? That which we call a rose by any other name would smell as sweet.") What I mean by one word, you mean by another.

A lot of people when they are giving advice are:-

1. Telling you what's best for them
2. Selling you shit
3. Sharing a lie or a practice that's holding them back, a lie or a practice they're holding onto like a life raft because it's got them this far and they're too scared to go any further

4. Telling you what they want

5. Sharing in a group delusion

6. Telling you to pursue an effect of success as a cause (it's not – and if you pick up certain habits, commitments, contracts before you are ready, you will find it extremely difficult to get to where you are going with them weighing you down). There is a reason they are called the "trappings" of success.

7. Ignorant to the fact that we can all succeed in different ways.

I'm going to use Christmas as an example:-

"You can't have Christmas without a tree." Yes you can.

"You have to give to charity at Christmas." No I don't.

"You have to see all your family at Christmas." I don't.

"You have to do Christmas cards."

"What's Christmas without a glass of Baileys?" Fine.

"You gotta be home for Christmas."

"Oh, it's a holiday, I know you're trying to be vegan but why don't you cut yourself some slack and enjoy the turkey?" Because, given time and money, I'd rather have a special vegan meal on Christmas, not the leftovers of what you choose to eat.

And actually for a lot of people it's not even a religious holiday because they don't believe in Jesus.

But hopefully you can see that if you buy into everybody's beliefs at Christmas (or, on the other hand, if you don't give new things a chance) you may not ever get to enjoy what you will discover is your perfect way to celebrate Christmas (and I do love Christmas).

If you want to go nuts and decorate your house with seventy five fibre optic Christmas trees and buy all your acquaintances lavish gifts, that's your choice, some years you need a little show.

To celebrate Christmas "properly" think of what the family of the baby Jesus had; no home, little money, a faithful little donkey, each other and a kind inn keeper, a very few guests, and then a hasty exit before the vengeful king could murder the baby. We'd judge that pretty harshly these days, but I think, as we look at nativity scenes around the world, in cribs and churches, in schools and homes, and hung on trees, in shops and all kinds of places, the very first Christmas was holier and more magical than many we have experienced in our lives.

Think back to moments of success in your life. Was there a parade? Lots of flashing lights? Were there press releases and announcements? Did you have a newsletter telling the world, a website? These are all fine things, but moments of success can also be private, confidential. Many of the greatest things we ever achieve we can't even explain why they meant so much to us.

Success can be instinctive, small, fleeting, precious and unwitnessed, it can be like a rainbow or a shooting star.

What is true for you about your success may not be true for anyone else in the world.

Fear of being, doing, having the very thing we want

I'm going to jump in at the deep end.

Recently, in my very humble lifestyle (any of you who may have read all my stories of lavish resorts and massages might like this bit), I was lying on a bottom bunk of a girl's dorm room in a youth hostel in London. It was clean, warm, dry and actually somewhere I've come to enjoy staying on a lot of occasions, and just before I went to sleep I felt a divine, warm feeling radiating out from my heart. It was joy.

I had no car, no high profile job, no money really, no boyfriend or significant other, no children, no house and yet I felt so happy, because I was free.

It wasn't just a freedom to go anywhere, to do anything, I think it was just a relief to be what I was, and to stop trying to be what I wasn't, and to know that I didn't need those things to make me happy.

So often we have to pretend. We pretend to be what we are not (especially if we are English) and we pretend for so long that we forget who we are – we become the mask, and it feels like the man in the iron mask, that we can't breathe, we can't feel the air on our face, that we are prisoners. So it was strange in the youth hostel to look up at the cross wires of the bunk above and think, well it's a bit like prison, but I am not in the prison I can make of my life.

I can find a million ways to entrap myself. A million rules, from the spiritual to the financial (some of which are fair enough, quite practical), but it is a constant battle between lies and the truth, between my ego and my spirit to say, "This is me, and this is what I can do today, and guess what, this is what I want to do today."

In the last few years I have been acutely aware of my needs, and I have learned to embrace them, most commonly my need for a bed for the night. It (as well as the occasional need for food, chargers, and so many practical things) has taken me to places I would never have thought to go, places it was impossible, too expensive, too weird and too wonderful to stay in. So far so good. Last week, looking for a bed for the night, I headed to Canterbury Youth Hostel to stay in a hobbit house, a little wooden pod with a bathroom and almost kitchen – my dream home, who could ask for anything more? Yet, somehow I found myself at the Cathedral, somehow I discovered that they offered pilgrim's blessings, and after debating with myself and my ego I let go of money (it's not cheap) and time (I really should be working) and asked to go in. (Turns out that pilgrims don't pay). It was exactly where I was meant to go, where I was meant to end up. I wept as I hoped that perhaps this was the end of a long and tiring journey, since I left my home of 22 years to go on the Camino de Santiago, whatever, it taught me that I was in exactly the right place again, and my need had brought me home.

My needs have brought me, over and over again back to where I am supposed to be, whether that is caring for a family member, counselling someone suffering or in need, or advising people on finishing and publishing their books. In each case, as we used to say in Zumba® Fitness, I was the student and the teacher. In each case my needs brought me back to me, to my true nature.

Why the long story? Because no matter how much I have tried over the years to be true to myself, to embrace success, I am so well trained to be what I am not and so afraid, that often the only things that really propel me forward in the right direction are primal needs and forces, that make me encounter my deeper fears when I feel I cannot fight the battle against my ego any longer.

Or to put it another way, things have to go wrong to get them to go right.

Perhaps one of the best stories that demonstrates this is "The Alchemist," the story of how one man has to travel, risk and give up everything he has in order to come back to the beginning and discover true riches.

So it is for most of us, our success, our glory, our true gifts are inside us all the time, so close we just cannot see them, although we feel them within us always, becoming heavier and heavier the less we use them.

We've been taught many things, but I believe that expressing our true nature, whether it is in business, management, art, music, speech, compassion or words, is the ultimate act of generosity, to share our true essence with the world, to serve the world, and in so doing we serve ourselves. Like animals, we crow not just to be a pain in the ass, but to wake people up. It's our job, and our nature.

If we are not what we are, we are something else, and if we don't have a very good reason for this, and if we don't have time to recover, we will suffer and get sick, physically, mentally and/or spiritually.

So why this terror at doing, being or having the thing that is true to us? I have often heard it said that it is not our fear, it is our ego's fear. That little imposter, that little parasite, the ego, the part of us that is simply made up in order to shield the real us from the world, for whatever reason. For us to be us, the ego has to go, and every step we take towards our true identity we lose the false identity.

Sometimes we are honestly two things (or more) or can do two (or more) things that seem at odds with each other. We could be a gold medallist in the Olympics and also transgender. So success in one thing seems to pull us further away from another thing that is true for us but which society tells us is incompatible.

Women who want children and to have careers, I don't think it's a question of "having it all," it's a question of being true to all the aspects of ourselves. Men who want to be nurses, which is now a commonplace situation in hospitals – but at one time would have been laughed at.

We are growing up in many ways in society, and outdated beliefs about our limitations are fading away. More and more people of different classes and backgrounds, and of course races and religions, are moving into roles that reflect the authenticity of their souls. Women become priests, and the lie that was held as truth for so long that these two things were incompatible fades away.

One small step for a transgender Olympian is a giant leap for mankind.

Before I go on, let me just say that many of the other fears of success I'm going to talk about can also be used by the ego to repress the true self, to stop us from doing our best, so before you wholeheartedly agree, "Yes, that's me," think twice, then think again, and then maybe just ignore me and go do it anyway.

In the words of Ray Bradbury, "Don't think about it, do it, then think about it."

Another element of our terror at doing, being or having the thing that we want is this; this is when we come alive, when we feel most truly ourselves. When we dance around the fire without fear we let go of our masks, and the imposter.

When we feel alive, we feel.

To be a decent writer, or painter or singer, we must feel (although maybe I'm wrong as there are so many who did some pretty good work while blind drunk). Stephen King talks about this a lot in "On Writing." Perhaps our need for anaesthesia comes from the opening up of wounds that comes as we tell stories, sing songs and put our hearts into anything we do. In the language of the Buddha and spiritual traditions, we awaken, or at least, the more we stay true to who and what we are, we stop pretending and start, like "The Velveteen Rabbit" to become real.

As a survivor of PTSD I wish I could say there was nothing to fear (I tell myself when going through an episode, "The only thing we have to fear is fear itself"), but what I can tell you is that the more times I ride out an episode, either caused by some obvious fear trigger or some less obvious success trigger, is that I get better and better at riding it out, like flu, or diarrhoea, or grief... and it's better out than in.

All it takes is practice.

What is fear?

Eh? Why am I asking this now? Shouldn't I have asked this at the beginning of the book?

Some fear researchers believe that there are primal, inherited, even racial fears and others learned in our lifetimes.

Some fear researchers believe that our fear stems from the panic of being left and the worry that there will be no one to take care of us, which comes from childhood fears of abandonment and separation.

Some will tell you a lot about our lizard brain.

Some say the other side of fear is love.

Some say the other side of love is love.

I have come to understand that I experience more than one type of fear.

The type of fear I experience during PTSD and similar episodes is not logical but is like something being released from my body. There are ways to try and calm it, but it's really like trying to ride out a storm, and just let it go. I feel this type of fear is like grief, something that has to be experienced in order to be released – you have to say hello before you can say goodbye, as my therapist taught me.

Then there are the mindfuck fears. The early in the morning, middle of the night, ego racing, trying to get me to stop or slow down or turn around because I am going in exactly the right direction for my authentic self.

Then sometimes they are accurate fears, where my mind puts two and two together and I realise I do need to worry and take action about something, or at least go walk along the beach and figure out my next step.

Then there is the "I love you" fear. The fear that comes from my ego, because it truly believes, like my family and some of my friends, that I need this, or have to have that, and this fear comes from a deep self-love, but it is a human, learned to protect me, sort of love, and so I just tell it, "Shhhh, it'll all be alright."

Through my travels I have learned not to be afraid, but to be wise, to have faith and do the right thing, even if on the surface it seems foolish, and to learn the difference between instinctive wisdom and deep rooted fear (whether it happens to be inherited or just learned really early on). To do my best to trust and not be afraid.

What is success?

The original subtitle of this book was "Getting Thin, Getting Rich and Getting Laid... What's The Problem?" Seen like that, what is the problem with success? And more relevantly, for this chapter – what is success?

It is different for everyone.

Fitness is different for lots of people. When I worked with people with multiple sclerosis the goal was just to have an enjoyable half hour, with friends, and maybe hold back some of the symptoms of the disease – we went way beyond that, and I don't recall anyone feeling intimidated by that success. But when I worked with more healthy people struggling to lose a few pounds that success brought immediate drama.

What's your definition of success? Why did you pick up this book? Maybe you don't know it yet in your conscious mind.

Do you dream of being rich and living in a big house, but can't commit to buying the big house? I will tell you that a big house can often have big problems and take big amounts of time to keep up. Is that truly what success means for you? I know that for me, at times, being able to rent a huge house has been exactly what I needed in my life, at other times, being able to afford even to stay in a hostel was perfect for where I needed to be and what I needed to be doing.

Would you like to find the partner of your dreams, have a baby, get laid? Anything is possible.

Would you like to be the person who discovers a new way to meditate, a new way to treat life-threatening illnesses, the person who discovers the secret of time travel or interplanetary travel? Do you want to be the person who wins the Tour de France honestly, a gold medal at the next Olympics, or the person who finally, once and for all, stops drinking, or leaves an abusive relationship?

I feel that this book is helping me to take a quantum leap in pursuing my goals in life, becoming what my soul strives to become, and that it will serve other people who struggle with success, who have learned unhealthy fears of their authentic success.

I hope that this book appeals to business people (isn't that all of us, even if we are just in the business of keeping the cupboard stocked and the wood for the fire stocked up). I hope it appeals to parents. I hope it appeals to carers. I hope it appeals to spiritual seekers. Because I see all of these people, especially the spiritual seekers, being sold a pack of lies and guided down dead ends.

I say this not out of ego, but out of awareness. I say this out of noticing, whenever I look for a guide or a teacher how often I find someone trying to persuade me to...

- listen to them because they've made a lot of money or people who are billionaires or millionaires rate them,
- listen to them because lots of famous people think they're great,
- let go of suspicion and listen without prejudice. To let them in the door before I have done my due diligence. (I did this once, with well known double glazing salespeople who then wouldn't leave my house),
- listen to them because they have achieved something extraordinary – because they have perfect health or can run fast,
- listen to them because they work with big corporates or governments, or charities.

These are not the questions I want to ask someone when I am looking for a guide, these are the questions (and they don't all have to be "yes" answers):

- Have you done this yourself?
- Have you done this for other people?
- Are you happy? Do you enjoy sharing this, teaching this… whether you make a lot of money or not?
- Is this, what you are doing and I am asking you to do for me, something that makes you shine?

43

Sometimes the answer is no, sometimes the question is more like:-

- Have you tried and failed to do this a hundred times?
- Have you made a lot, maybe even all the mistakes there are to make in this?
- Are you still struggling, is this still an everyday challenge?
- Do you know how it feels to be like me, struggling, suffering to get past this thing I want to do?
- Can you treat me with compassion and consideration as I struggle through what should be easy – can you be kind?

For me in the last year, success was remaining kind, success was letting go, success was surrendering to being and doing whatever other people needed me to be, success was saying, "I can't cope," and asking for help, success was doing more than I could or should have done, in order to fail, to learn, success was making more money than I ever thought I could doing something I loved, success was being honest and letting others help me, being vulnerable, success was pushing myself to the limit of what my skill and intelligence could do as an author, success was leaving, success was coming back, and all of this success was built on the years of previous successes, and failures, which were also success, because they were me learning what works in different situations.

Success was being human. It was not sitting in a cave meditating or seeking bliss.

For me, a few years ago, success was opening the door to my grief, and spending time healing, grieving, learning complete acceptance and practising unconditional love, so that when the time came to be there for someone it was with acceptance, not struggling, still carrying my grief. Success, and it is a huge success, was that I had let go of the past.

What is success? I say it is feeling real emotions everyday, because this is how we are successfully human. And our journey is not to be robots, or gods, because, say it with me now;

"We are not human beings on a spiritual journey, we are spiritual beings on a human journey."

I am tired of spiritual gurus offering perfect health if I just manifest it. I have come to understand that my illnesses are perfect and often serve my spirit in ways I can only begin to understand. Buddha was fat.

I am tired of business gurus offering financial abundance, sometimes we learn more and are served more by lack. Sadhguru walks around without a penny in his pocket (don't worry, I'll take your money – I'm not a nun).

I am tired of being asked to boost my Instagram following when I know I always have the perfect audience. (I could tell you stories.)

Thich Nhat Hanh says that the miracle is not to walk on water, it is to walk on the green earth knowing that you are walking on the green earth.

Your success is within you, whether it is the perfection of eating an orange as described by this Buddhist master in his books, so that you truly appreciate and taste it, or just pressing your feet into the warm sand, or hugging your grandma. And feeling it.

Success is mastering freedom, authenticity, all these big concepts, learning to live your life as you.

But before you get all "the best you," "your best life," "a better you," on me, let me tell you a secret.

You are perfect.

Your struggle is perfect.

Your rate of growth is perfect.

An acorn is perfect. An oak tree is perfect. There is not one moment between the moment this entity is a tiny acorn, and when it is an enormous thousand year old oak tree, that has absorbed all kinds of other matter in order to become an oak tree, that it is not perfect.

Every microsecond of this tree's life is perfect. From when it cannot grow due to drought, from when someone pots

46

it up and forgets about it in the back of a shed, from when it is almost killed off by the cold in the winter... but what there is, is tension. Inside the acorn something strives to be more, something dreams of more, something knows, given the right moisture and earth that it can be something incredible, this acorn yearns to be more than it is.

The acorn's journey is perfect. The acorn's impatience is perfect, the desire is perfect, the yearning is perfect.

I know that you are a successful human being because you are alive, and because the sperm that created you beat out, I don't know, five million other sperm to become you. You have already defied all the odds, you have already succeeded and achieved the dream of the sperm you once were, before you could think, before you met the egg, before you were you...

Perhaps you just stopped by this book to be reminded, because that fire, that life, that yearning is still within you.

You are perfect, and that perfection will continue to unfold naturally, if it takes you time to remember what nourishes you, which way is up, perhaps you need that time, but if now is the time to rise, and you know it, then don't be afraid.

If you came here today to find a way to escape your fear of success well, you came to the right place, at the right time. (Which is also success.)

47

Fear of making mistakes

There are none.

Fear of false success

I told my girlfriend when we first started dating that I didn't want kids or to get married, but now she and everyone we know is pressurising me to tie the knot and have two kids and a dog.

Say it again. And again. And again.

It is not your job to be what someone else wants you to be.

It's okay for her to change her mind about what she was happy with from when she met you until now. But you do not have to accommodate that.

If she wants something you cannot or do not want to give, she has to decide whether to stay with you.

It happens all the time.

But if you want to change your mind, you are free to do that too.

I started the degree that my parents wanted me to do and funded me for, but now I just can't imagine working in a corporation or a laboratory my whole life.

Read "The Four Agreements" by Don Miguel Ruiz. Think about what you have agreed to, and what you have not. You have a right to change your mind, it is up to you and your family to decide if it is appropriate for you to pay them back. In any case, whatever agreements and promises we make, we cannot know how we are going to feel until we walk the walk. You are not a slave and you are responsible for your own life.

I love what I do, but an opening has come up in management... well, what I mean is that the manager left and I've been acting manager for ages, but I don't really want to do that job – I want to stay doing what I love.

Those sneaky bastards. I bet they're not paying you the extra money either for the senior role.

No one can force you. Say what you want and be prepared to leave.

There are many business concepts that are outdated and untrue. These have even been written into books about running your own business and about entrepreneurship, but it doesn't make them true.

One of the biggest of these is that we all want the senior role, and that somehow we have to train others to do the job we used to do. In some cases, this is like asking the first chair violin in a symphony to become the conductor, and then go teach the oboe player to become a better violinist (can you imagine, the new conductor gritting his or her teeth every time they have to listen to the solo being murdered by a less talented musician?) Many of the things we do are an art, a gift. We are not robots, and many of these business concepts are hangovers from a factory age... an age of producing the same thing over and over, an age of "skill" being synonymous with ability to push buttons, an age of people having to work within specific time frames or shifts, instead of according to natural rhythms.

Is this fear of success or fear of promotion away from the thing we are successful at?

Only you can truly know in any of these situations if this is fear of success or fear of false success – only your heart can tell you which is your way.

I am scared that if I am successful I won't have time for my family.

Once, I was thinking of going into business with my boyfriend. Things were so difficult because we were so stretched, and so the idea of working together seemed like a perfect solution. And I went to a business event, where a husband and wife who had a coaching partnership were doing a session with Q&A. So I asked the question, "Is it a good idea?"

The husband was quiet for a moment and then answered with absolute honesty. He said, you and your partner will either have problems because you don't spend enough time together because you're working apart, or you will have problems because you spend too much time together because you're working together.

This, my year of failure (and success), has shown me that my failure may have been the answer to my family's prayers – so that I could be around for them. And I am so glad that I was, I am so grateful to have been in that position. And yet. My failure would not have continued to make them happy.

Being successful enough to say no to some work, to be able to rent a place near to them for Christmas, to come… and go… makes them and me happy.

I am in awe of the people who work minimum wage jobs, even just one, and then there are the people who work two or three to support their families, to be there for them. Then there are people who work soul destroying corporate jobs to provide their kids with everything. I know that they are all trying to do the right thing.

I want to create my own work/life balance and part of that is saying yes and no to work opportunities and commitments. Remembering that I am the boss of me.

The real question is, can you resist the temptation? Can you stand up to the lie that you have to do this or do that, can you say, "No, I'm sorry I'm taking my mum to the hospital?"

Or can you say to your family, "No, I'm sorry, I'm working?"

the reversal – a note

When we go our own way it takes everything sometimes to resist the everyday "wisdom" of society, friends, colleagues, family telling us how we must live our lives. "You need this, you need that, you need whatever…"

"No I don't."

Until I do.

Habits are the enemy. Because when we live out a habit we do so automatically, without questioning.

When we practice, as we must do, eventually our practice becomes rote, becomes stale, stagnant, because we are not questioning it, not asking, is this right for me today?

If you think about some popular spiritual challenges:-

"Do one thing every day that scares you."

"Do the thing you cannot do."

"Try, try and try again."

"Walk a different way to work."

These are all about breaking habits.

Resisting popular wisdom can also become habit – ignoring the person who keeps telling you how to live your life or who wants to judge or approve every detail of your life can become a negative habit, becomes sometimes (even accidentally) they get it right.

If you look at our political parties in the UK, it sometimes seems that their job is to oppose and argue every possible idea or action – but even they agree on certain things, especially coming up to an election.

Sometimes agreeing is okay.

Fear of consequences of success

What we see of success is often polarised between "Hello" magazine and "Isn't life glamorous!" which often makes us think that success is just having a new kitchen, and tabloid hell journalism where every slightly famous person has a "drug hell", "adultery hell", "mental health disorder hell", "bulimia hell"... is it any wonder we're scared of success?

I hate the chaos that comes with building work and decorating (I can just about do Christmas decorations) and I don't want any kind of "party hell" in my life. My ego screams, "I JUST WANT THINGS TO STAY THE SAME!"

I have had my dream project turned into fodder for a Sunday tabloid. I know that there are people who say that these stories are made up with the people in them – let me tell you, we did not want this story and we did not expect it. My name wasn't even mentioned, the pictures looked gorgeous, it wasn't even that bad a story, and yet... it really hurt. I was in shock. Something I had worked so hard on, a project I believed in and that was something so beautiful to us, was turned into sometimes tawdry and tacky to sell newspapers. This is not success. This is what happened to me at school when I had my first boyfriend, and rumours started circulating, because rumours are like ghosts – you can't fight them. And suddenly you can't hold hands in the playground because people will think you're doing it. You can't relax and just be yourself because everyone's watching.

Oscar Wilde once said, "The only thing worse than being talked about is not being talked about."

Sometimes the lies and the mud that gets slung when you're doing well can be so toxic that it's tempting to hide, to lie down in the grass and never get up. But that's how bullies win. That's how those who are less talented cut you down – and I've said it before and I'll say it again, you don't serve people by letting them abuse you. So if nothing else, do it for the bullies, do it so that they do not win, do it as an act of kindness to them, because if they win, they lose.

Jealousy and hatred

Hatred isn't real. But jealousy, is that real? We say that all negative emotions are rooted in fear, so what does someone who is jealous truly fear?

- Being left behind.
- Being found out as not good enough themselves.
- Having to change and move on if they are ousted.
- Their own success.

I'm going to talk later about jealousy as a solution to fear of success (yes, really) and also about competition, but let's for a moment talk about pure, open, green eyed monster jealousy that can be extremely detrimental to both the focus of the emotion and the person feeling it. (Is it me that feels a hint of anger within jealousy also?)

Shakespeare wrote a great play about jealousy: "Othello". In it, Iago, twisted up in his own desires (and jealousy) uses doubt and lies to convince Othello that his wife is unfaithful to him. He knows exactly how to twist the knife, to the point that Othello finally kills his wife and then takes his own life. When I talk later about jealousy as solution you'll see how we can untangle this if it is our own jealousy – but what about if it is their jealousy? How can we shield ourselves from the kind of emotion that causes someone to destroy something if they can't have it for themselves?

If Dorothy could have taken off the ruby slippers in "The Wizard of Oz" and handed them over to The Wicked Witch of The West, she would have. And so would we, about many of the things we have that others want. Would we give our height away, our abilities? Guess what, scientists found a way for me to give my brother a kidney (but, of course, that wasn't in response to jealousy). I believe that there is a reason we have all been given our own gifts, and so if we want to give them away, we have to find ways to share them – if we can make beautiful music we need to find ways to share that, either by teaching others, or recording albums, performing live - as someone very wise once said, "You only get to keep what you give away". But the more we give away, the more jealousy we can sometimes inspire.

Have we all had the friend who we try to help, maybe we give them money, maybe we give them stuff, maybe we give them time, maybe we try to teach them what we can do, maybe we support them in their projects, maybe we go out with them when we really don't want to because we feel a little bit sorry for them… and they always want… just a little bit more.

And then you notice a little something in their demeanour, a little resentment, a little "well, it's alright for you". When you're healthy, "well, it's alright for you," and you feel you have to apologise for not being unwell.

When you go to pay the check and there's no argument, no "let me," like there used to be. When your stuff or your services are just taken for granted, because "we're friends".

When you're trying to follow your dreams and instead of urging you on, they whisper negatives, or tell you it'll never work, or "why would you want to do that?"

When you're off to study or write and they shrug about working on their own book and say, "Oh well, I'll sit down and write it all in one go sometime," when they've never finished writing a book before.

When you mention getting off on the finer points of punctuation (or something geeky in your own field) and they say, "Get a life."

When you say, "Guess what, I'm an Amazon Best Seller in Meditation!"

And they say, "But are you making any money?"

When they say, "Writing some more books that no one is ever going to read?"

When they say, "Maybe you could write a real book one day."

And then, when we try to slow down or stop the slide, comes the backlash.

When we say, "Can I have my books back?"

"Oh, are those your books? I thought that was a gift."

When we all work on a project together and they don't pull their weight and get upset when you mention it, and suddenly you feel like you're the one in the wrong.

When they make social plans for you and get upset when you say no, (like when they decide that you really want to spend time with their boyfriend).

When we say, "I'm sorry but I just cannot have this conversation again, if you want to start your own business you need to go do it and stop asking me to set it up for you."

And then comes the *real* backlash. When it becomes clear that they never had any intention of paying you back, or giving you back your DVD, when it becomes clear that they were quite happy to sit on your coat tails and let you run things.

When it becomes clear that in a twisted way they thought they *were* you, and your success was theirs.

Brené Brown calls a lot of what she does "Defence against the Dark Arts," so can we defend against jealousy, can we fight it, or do we do as our teachers and parents told us at school and just rise above?

Awareness as always is key. Learning who we can and cannot trust. Shonda Rhimes writes beautifully about this in her book "Year of Yes". The first time she realised she had a situation along these lines and "broke up" with a friend it hurt. It hurt bad. And then the next time, less so…

The first time I felt like I had to break up with a friend like this it was as bad as a serious romantic break up, there was no clean cut, there was a backwards and forwards as I asked for space, and then had to admit that the toxic relationship was having a negative impact on the rest of my life. If she had been obsessed with me, I was now obsessed with the situation.

A few times later I walked away from another friend with hardly a backward glance. The situation was different and the incident that sparked the break up more immediate, but at the same time I knew where it was going. I had been down this road before.

We live and we learn.

Jealousy is toxic, so we have to be aware of it, and when someone in our lives cannot handle our success we may have to lose them. But first, just be aware of it. Just listen to the words coming out of their mouth. In the words of many shaman, "If you listen, people will tell you who they are." When somebody says something that eats away at your confidence, pay attention. In "Bridget Jones: The Edge of Reason" Helen Fielding calls them jellyfishers, "She's a jellyfisher: You have a conversation with her that seems all nice and friendly, then you suddenly feel like you've been stung and you don't know where it came from."

I remember a friend of mine who always used to get asked out by the hottest guys, everyone knew she was the beauty. When we went out and met two guys I was extremely chatty with the super good looking one, expecting him to go for her. He didn't. He went for me. Afterwards I said to her, "I can't believe he's interested in me, he's sooooo hot."

"Oh no," she told me confidentially, "I'm not surprised... I see really hot guys with plain girls all the time."

Note to self; this friendship has a short shelf life.

I'm not going to try to tell you that a real friendship doesn't have bumps in the road, mistakes and things said that can't be unsaid, but I think real friendships survive, family relationships can come back from the dead, even though we make mistakes like this, even though sisters in particular can say the cruellest things out of jealousy. "In Her Shoes" is a great film about this. But it's a bit like cutting into an apple, sometimes there's a little bad bit, even a bug, but sometimes when you cut it into it, you know it's not even worth trying to salvage.

Jealousy is toxic and, yes, it is dangerous. Do not take it lightly, listen, pay attention and then, if necessary, run for your life. Remember Desdemona. (Othello's wife.)

And more importantly, remember that their jealousy is their problem, not yours. (But you know, don't be a dick about it, nobody needs someone turning up at their hospital bed telling them how great they feel – but remember, if you weren't well you couldn't visit them at all).

If I am successful and make lots of money, how will I know if someone loves me for me or for what I have, conversely what if the person I want to be with is intimidated by my success and the fact that I make more money than them?

I have fallen so low that I was able to see that someone loved me only for me. And I know it and will always know it. But I really should have known it all along.

They say that money is the root of all evil; it can certainly be the source of much confusion.

The person who loves you may even believe themselves that they love you for your money, that they are with you because of what you can provide. But it doesn't mean that it is true.

I have been rich and I have been poor.

I have been poor and thought rich, and rich and thought poor. I have walked like a pauper and seen the view from there, and also seen the view from the fanciest spots (sometimes for free).

Sometimes people are affectionate and helpful because they think you're broke, other times because they think you can help them and, very often, they don't even know what their motives are.

I say open your heart, and listen to it, even if you decide not to open your wallet.

Sometimes financial struggles, up or down, can be nature's way of testing us and the people around us, so it's okay to be a little Zen about it, a little experimental, allow things to happen and pay attention to your reactions and the reactions of those around you. What would you not do, no matter how poor you are? What would you not buy, no matter how rich you are?

If I am rich I will turn into an arsehole, and have to pay a lot of tax.

Try it and find out. Keep an eye on the turning into an arsehole thing and hopefully you won't (I find that the universe has a way of making sure you retain your humility, if you slip).

Read the chapter on Humility and hopefully you will see that if you are not serving just money on your way to success you won't stray too far from your path.

If I am successful I will lose friends and maybe alienate family.

Yes you will.

I'm so sorry, I wish I could say, "No, it'll be alright and nothing will change." But you would know I was lying. Wouldn't you?

An alcoholic who gives up drinking will be told that they have to stop socialising with the people they used to drink with. Even if you cut back, you might find it hard to be around people who still have habits you've let go. They might find it hard to be around you. They may resent you. They may think you think you're better than them.

I'm sorry.

Tony Robbins talks a lot about identity, Don Miguel Ruiz talks about labels. When you are the fat one of the group, what happens when you lose weight? Not only does your identity shift, but so does that of everyone in the group. Why do you think so many people put weight back on? It is easier to stay there than to make significant changes.

Why does Zumba work as a weight loss program or a fitness program where so many others fail? Because it doesn't just give you weight loss (or me rather), it brings joy.

When I took the class as a participant it was like it wiped a little hour clean of all the negative emotions, which began a shift to clearing out the rest of my life. It had made a clean spot, where I could see out of the window, and I wanted to see everything. It gave me hope.

But... I have had so many participants come once and... shine. Light up like it was Christmas, tell me how much they loved it, tell me they would see me next week and every week... and I never saw them again. My theory is that they saw that little clean spot, and then they took another look at the whole window, and they figured it would be easier to let it get dirty again than to clean the whole thing. If they carried on being joyful and happy, they might have to give up the rest of their lives. (I know I did.)

What happens when you get thin? When you get rich? When you fall in love?

Negativity. Jealousy. Fear. Resentment.

You. Rocked. The. Boat.

Sometimes you will have to terminate a relationship. If they can't handle the truth, sometimes it is the only way.

Sometimes you will have to take a step back. But please, take it back away from the person, not from your success, not from your true goals, not from being who you are. You will be surprised what people can and do adapt to when they realise you are not going back in your hole. Most people, and the most important people in your life, will get with the program. Some will become your biggest supporters given time. Some will say, "I always knew you had it in you."

And some you will beat your head against like a brick wall for the rest of your life. Because you choose to. And that's okay too. You can love and accept someone just the way they are, even if they cannot accept and love you. You just might need to take a lot of breaks from them... or you will end up with a very sore head.

One thing I will tell you which I said to a friend in a moment of wisdom when he was complaining about his mother's reaction to a big change in his career (and to be honest, some of it was societal too, she had to deal with some backlash from her friends and neighbours). I said, "You've been telling her who you are your whole life, and now you're telling her you're someone completely different. Have patience. You've been lying to her your whole life, so yeah, she feels betrayed, so be kind, it's hard on her too."

I wish I was so wise in the moments when it's my family and me.

But please remember, the whole, "If I change I'll lose all my friends and family" is also a great ego lie to hold you back from moving towards success. They may all just smile and nod, "Yeah, so what?!"

It could happen.

Another thing that could happen is that your success gives them permission to pursue their own success. (Which is probably why so many people react badly to it in the first place.)

If I succeed I will have to move on to the next level.

Yes.

This is very different from the false fear of "I have to become a manager".

No one ever said to Stephen King, "Oh, now you're such a successful and talented writer you should go train a whole load of other writers to write for you." But even Stephen King has to finish the book he is working on, no matter how much he is enjoying it, and move on to the next one, or to the next challenge in his life.

Again, if success means moving on to a different challenge, another way of being, doing, having, there is a reason for that, and you will find joy in the next level, the next stage, even if you look back and miss the way things were. Nothing stays the same forever.

(See also The Way and How do you survive success?)

Fear of loss of success

I was dating.

I knew this because my therapist and I had spent time working out what I was doing.

"I'm dating." Whether or not I was actually seeing someone, I was open, I was, maybe not ready, but ready to be ready.

And then I started dating. The actual person who I was crazy about. Someone who had been in my vicinity for years, driving me nuts... because he had a girlfriend, and he wasn't the kind of guy who did stuff with someone else when he had a girlfriend, which, of course, made me want him more. And then we were at a dinner party and he was casually talking about breaking up with his girlfriend.

"I don't want another girlfriend." He was clear, he was going travelling. And yet.

I had to talk myself into it. I wanted to run. He wasn't serious, he wasn't boyfriend material, but... I had run away too many times. And besides, he'd left his bag behind. (Years later I'd see this move in "How To Lose A Guy In 10 Days" and wonder just how accidental it was.)

But I was dating. This was practice. I had rejected every other man for the last ten years because they weren't perfect. Well, he wasn't perfect, but I had to get back on the horse sometime.

It all went well, casual, jokey texts and emails, stupid things, great food, but then I did a really stupid thing. I fell in love. And I think he did too.

So I ran.

And I felt awful.

The old me would have got drunk, bitched about him to my friends and snogged someone else.

But the new me (after I'd done that, and upset several of my good friends by being too drunk to get to their birthday parties), stayed in therapy, and one afternoon, when things were slow at work, downloaded a long, long quiz on relationships and... fear of success.

Somewhere in the test, the penny dropped, I'd run away because what if it went right? If it went right I was risking so much, I was risking feeling like this, but so much worse, but the other truth in there, was that I was risking feeling what I was already feeling, down deep inside, some feelings that I had buried long ago, when my father died.

I texted him, I apologised, I asked him out again.

I did the right thing.

And then 7/7 happened, and I woke up with PTSD.

People say that to have a child is to have your heart walking around outside of your body.

I know, as is so beautifully expressed in e e cummings' poem, "i carry your heart with me(i carry it in" that we are all connected, that whatever our individual hearts experience is felt by all of us, whether that is a lover, husband, brother, mother, grandmother. No one who has sat by the side of someone they loved having chemo can tell me different. It is the best place and the worst place, and it can take what feels like superhuman courage to keep our hearts open during these times, to just keep loving in the face of illness and ageing. It is an act of heroism to love someone with a terminal illness, but it is also an act of heroism to love someone who could walk out of your house and get hit by a bus.

We did get back together, even though he was leaving, we did have perfect moments, and we did say goodbye, and I believe we did give each other something very special over the next few years as we stayed in touch. Perhaps for me, what I really learned, was that I could love and lose, and still survive.

So I kept loving, (and dating) and losing, and surviving, and one day I was strong enough to sit down and start to grieve for all the many losses I experienced when I was younger, one day I was strong enough to finally begin to let go of what I had lost, decades before.

If that was too deep for you, let me tell you another story.

I got thin. Really thin. (It was actually about the time I was dating that guy I told you about – and yes, it was because someone was going to see me naked. I didn't see him as often as I'd have liked, he was always doing something or going somewhere, so I went to the gym).

I was at my ideal weight.

I ran on the treadmill for hours each week. I had fruit on my desk at work (I only allowed myself to eat crisps or a bar of chocolate if I had eaten two pieces of fruit first). I ate healthily. I got home and didn't sit down, just grabbed my gym bag and went straight there.

I got up before 6am and went to the gym where I stood inside, waiting for them to let us go through the turnstiles, with the other early morningers. We never made eye contact.

It was hard work.

I threw away or gave away all my fat clothes. I got to wear lovely, skinny things.

I remember thinking one day that I would never get pregnant, because I couldn't face trying to lose the weight again – the maintenance of just staying thin was so hard.

Then I met a guy. We went out for dinner, we cooked together, we drank wine, and beer, and we ate breakfast in bed. I got fat, he got really fat, but we were happy and in love.

When he left, at first I couldn't eat, but after a year or more all I could do was eat. I got fat, then fatter, then fatter still. I was miserable in my job, which revolved around the biscuit tin, and although I ran on the treadmill I was at crunch time. I was filling out size 18 trousers (size 22 in the US) and it was time to either buy the biggest sized trousers I'd ever bought in my life, or do SOMETHING.

Something happened. Something called... Zumba.

Everything changed.

I made eye contact with people in the gym, they knew me, we laughed, I *ran* from the office to get home on time. I stopped eating biscuits because I couldn't dance with a belly full of biscuits. I fell in love. With dance. With the way I could move my body. (Maybe a little bit with my gay instructor.) And one day I got so sad at the end of the class that I realised it was the best part of my week, and I realised how miserable the rest of my life was...

I quit my job, became an instructor, and more and more and more...

Zumba changed my life.

And I know that all I ever need to do to lose weight is to do a little dance, make a little love... get down tonight.

The answer was right there within me all the time.

Do I worry about getting pregnant or putting on weight? No. Because I found my way.

And I cannot lose my way, it's part of me.

And so I know all the answers. Yeah, right. Even the Dalai Lama doesn't have all the answers. And he had it easy... taken away from his family when he was very young, letting go of attachment to family or friends, taught to love within a sangha, a community so you never get too attached to one person, his Buddhist oaths make it easy – no lovers to get hung up on. (Okay, I'm kidding – but there is a reason that many Buddhist monks are remote figures.)

Even Thich Nhat Hanh (whose sangha I have studied with) talks about how difficult it is to make romantic attachments, and then let go. He has two books about romantic love that are worth their weight in gold. But here's a thing. When he set up his community in France, he turned to his students/disciples, eight people – four men, four women (very equal opportunities) and he said, right, now we are going to create our own way of doing things, so you get to choose, you can either be celibate or you can get married or have a committed relationship, just as long as you all honour sex as a sacred part of life. All the women chose to be single, all the men chose to get married.

Here's another thing. Bhutan is one of the most Buddhist countries in the world, often called Shangri-La or the happiest place on earth. Their monks are allowed to get married. And their culture is polygamous.

Some say, "desire is the design flaw". I disagree (and so do many Buddhist teachers). What the problem is, is attachment to desire.

A wonderful teacher on attachment is Don Miguel Ruiz Jr. (check out his book "The Five Levels of Attachment," which I highly recommend) but here is a short explanation.

I breathe in. I breathe out.

As soon as I start to worry about breathing it becomes more shallow, laboured, I start to fantasise about pain in my chest, the air quality, am I getting sick?

I hold my breath. My ribs become stiff. My muscles clench.

Asleep, I breathe normally, unconsciously, I breathe deeply, I don't have to do the thousands of breathing exercises in yoga practices.

When I get out in nature I feel at peace, I trust my surroundings and I breathe in the smell of the sea, the trees, the earth, the mountains.

It is easy. It is not easy. We all have to find our own way, what works for us, but I believe that what is meant for us will come to us easily, and that the best way of messing it up is to hold onto it too tightly, to be rigid.

We may love, and lose, we may have money, and lose it, we may get slim – into perfect fitness and health, and then get sick, we may have respect from our peers, win awards, and then lose that, we may buy a brand new car and then have an accident, but perhaps when life takes away from us, there is a reason, maybe many, and perhaps one of those reasons is to teach us what is important, what is real, what is true to our nature, what makes us happy, what we can live without, and what we choose not to live without, who is with us when we are at our lowest and perhaps most importantly, how to let go.

When we let go of everything, when we set everything we hold onto free, we will discover what we can never lose, because it is a part of us, and what was never ours in the first place.

The Wall

In marathon running there is a moment that they call "the wall". It is a physical, mental and spiritual barrier. It is when all the pain is felt, when the mind starts to believe in failure, that the run will never end, it feels like there is nothing left.

In coaching other authors there is always a moment when they hit the wall. I think this is the difference between writing a book and anything else (like articles or blogs), this is the reason that people are in awe of it. It's not difficult – it's just like running 26 and a bit miles, but it's not the writing or the running that scares people, it's the wall.

The wall makes you naked. It's the moment when you have to go on when you can't go on. It's the moment you break through your lies, when you know that you always had it in you, that it is easy, in the moment of encountering and going over the wall the truth is that the barrier is just our ego.

The battle is always between the authentic self and the ego self. The moment of truth is the best and the worst part of the marathon, of the Camino, of the book, of the relationship, of producing a movie, it is crunch time, and it is when you can't hide anymore.

People let us down, we let ourselves down, we make mistakes, and the wall is what stands between "I'm going to run the marathon" and "I ran the marathon". It's what happens somewhere in the exam room, when we either have it, or we don't.

In a marathon it's pretty obvious when someone starts going the wrong way. Not so with a book. With a book, or a business, or a relationship, you can go backwards and forwards for days, months, years... a lifetime. You can pace, when all you need to do to succeed is to just keep putting one foot in front of the other.

Just... go.

(N.B. The wall is a lot like touching the void, which I wrote about in my book on being a live kidney donor, but it is not the same.)

Solutions

Top Ways to Escape Fear of Success

I have written more than nine books about the journey, with many, many practices for escaping fear of success. I'm not going to rewrite it all here, but just give you the main ones I use to this day (the others may work better for you, this is just the tip of the iceberg).

Go on a wing and a prayer

Stepping out, like Indiana Jones in "Indiana Jones and The Last Crusade" (which actually wasn't the last crusade) into the unknown, with nothing but faith, can be nature's way, like a bird being nudged out of the nest. Life will direct you to what you are afraid to experience – either what we might call darkness or what we might call light. Sometimes intuition calls us to our greatest defeats as well as our greatest successes – because it is the failures, the "mistakes," that we need to learn from in order to become who we are meant to be, or that we need to live through in order to be there, in service to others.

Don't think about it. Do it. Then think about it.

Sometimes I have struggled with an objective, a dream and then given up and gone to bed, feeling that I would never get there, I would never have the energy, the wherewithal – and then I wake up and go do it before I even have breakfast. If I had known, when I went to bed, I might have tossed and turned all night, I might have been stressed and nervous. Instead it was a surprise attack on "the enemy", on my ego, and instead of arguing with my thoughts and my mind, I just took action.

Let go of fear

It seems nonsensical to say that to let go of fear we must let go of fear. And yet, it is true. What I am really saying is that rather than "feeling the fear and doing it anyway" we can strive to not feel the fear in the first place.

We do this by silencing the mind, finding the space between the thoughts, drowning thoughts in music and traditional rhythms where the language of the lyrics is incomprehensible and therefore cannot mislead us. This is the goal of meditation, to perceive truth, which is not fear, to let go of notions, our illusions, that which we have been taught to fear. In the moment before I gave my brother a kidney, when fear disappeared, I could see the whole process for what it was, a miracle, so beautiful, so magical.

If we could see our lives like this, and let go, knowing that there will be pain and darkness, there will be struggle, but letting go of useless suffering and worry and doubt, how much bliss and joy would inhabit our days?

And for those of you who care about the answer to the question about why writers may be the most challenged of all, it is this. If I dance I can block out my thoughts with music, if I walk I can be present with nature, but here, right now, I have to work with words, and so it is harder to switch off my mind, the thoughts, my ego because it loves language, because that is how it lies to me the most. But it is doable. (It's just harder when I am editing.)

Do the thing you cannot do

Sometimes we do something extraordinary. So many retreats have incredible experiences, like fire walking or jumping off things, even massages... and these work, sometimes as part of the process, but sometimes just to teach us that nothing is impossible, that these "acts of power" break beliefs that we are small or weak, and so by doing one impossible thing we free ourselves to do the next. Do the thing you cannot do. Do not listen to your mind when it says it is impossible.

Be the storyteller

In training with Don Miguel Ruiz and his sons they use a powerful practice called recapitulation. You can actually do it every day, at the end of each day, walk through your life and look at every moment of your story, everything you told yourself, and in that way you can stalk your reactions, look at whether you have made assumptions, if your speech was impeccable, if you took things personally, you can see how you

85

told your story today. In Teotihuacan we walked in silence and we recapitulated our whole lives, paying attention to all the facts and fiction: what was real, what was imagined, how had we twisted things around, either to make ourselves the villain or the hero?

You will see in this book how often I have looked at a societal concept and held it up and said, eloquently, "Nah." And every time I do that, every time I talk to others about these lies in our reasoning, they agree with me. And then they go right back to living by these broken rules again. (And I try not to.)

You will see in this book how many times I have held up a lie I told myself, and looked at it from all angles, like looking at a black diamond, until I realised it was not a diamond, not even coal, not even sand, just a trick of the light (or the dark).

When we examine our stories, we break down the doors to our success, we break down our limiting beliefs, we break down societal lies (like apartheid or sexism) that hold us back, we review our family myths and tribal prejudices, and if we have the will and the energy, we can shatter the ones which betray us.

The Way

Ultimately the only way to get over fear of success is to be successful. To acclimatise. Or to get altitude sickness and go back down the mountain and try again (maybe it's not your mountain). In the end the mountain chooses you.

Once upon a time, as I travelled by bus around Mexico (the bit dangerous but not terribly dangerous part), I told the story of Alex in "Grey's Anatomy" who became terrified of elevators (or lifts as we call them) and so he had to have someone to ride up and down in the elevator with him until it just got boring.

I hope your success doesn't become boring for you, I think if it does you will always be able to find a new challenge if you try. But you know, sometimes a little boredom isn't the worst thing in the world. In fact, if you call it peaceful, if you call it rest, it's rather nice. As another doctor, McDreamy put it in (you've guessed it) "Grey's Anatomy" after he'd almost destroyed his life chasing his career, "When did saving a life stop being enough?"

On another part of my journey I sat and looked over the mountains after sleeping in a treehouse and remarked that the best coffee in the world was just whatever you drank in a place like that. A month later I was caning for my exact favourite coffee from my exact favourite store. We breathe in, we breathe out. If we recognise when comfort has gone, as Kahlil Gibran said, from the guest to the host, to the master, we can pull the rug right out from underneath it - stay in a Youth Hostel, get cold and wet on a beach and eat stale sandwiches. We can reconnect with life and remember what it feels like to get wet and muddy. Success perhaps is like that comfort, something we need to enjoy and let go of, breathe in, breathe out.

As soon as we reach the top of the mountain we need to get down again (see also "Life is My Sherpa").

Imposter Syndrome

Maya Angelou once described imposter syndrome as the feeling that one day everyone would figure out she was a fraud. Every book she released she felt that she'd got away with it, that one day they'd realise she couldn't really write.

For around three years I would occasionally look around the hall where I was teaching Zumba for the real teacher.

I think of Harry Potter mistaking the figure on the side of the lake for his own father, because he didn't recognise himself or his own abilities.

When I have sold a lot of books in a month I always think that they've bought them by mistake, and am half waiting for an email to say, "Sorry, we need to refund these books."

I have been in Rome for three days. Each day it feels a little more real.

Is Imposter Syndrome just a way of acclimatising to our success? Just a way of getting used to a new situation? Is it letting go of the habit of being less than we are, or being the student and learning the habit of being the teacher? Is it just adjusting? Is it a safety feature of the way our mind, body and soul work to prevent us climbing too high too fast? Or a way of maintaining humility as we grow and excel?

Is the way to counteract it perhaps to live into things, or to overstate our abilities, like Muhammad Ali, "I am the greatest, I said that even before I knew I was."

Or can we just ignore it and get on with what we are doing? Is it a natural protection from some of the fear of success, a form of denial that protects us as we move forward, because… as I say in another part of this book, "Challenging fear of success is a grief process." Is Imposter Syndrome just another word for denial?

Is Imposter Syndrome, the problem, part of the solution, or part of the origin of the problem, or all three?

Imposter Syndrome as Solution:-

Muhammad Ali said, "I am the greatest, I said that even before I knew I was." We see this way of thinking in mantras and forms of manifesting. Some might call it wishful thinking, I feel there is definitely a moment when the universe wants us to get off our arse and "manifest" a cup of tea by putting the kettle on. We live into the life, the state of being we want to achieve. As I said at the beginning of this book, and as they say at the beginning of the Camino, the only way is to start.

But what about disbelief and fear as motivators? What about the times when the most incentivising thing a person can do to us is to say, "You will never do this." What about when the disbelief that we will achieve something, the not knowing is as important as the self-belief or knowing?

What about every moment in (almost) every romantic comedy when the breach between two people is so bad that it has to get worse... one is about to get on a plane, to get married, to take the job or leave the job, or my favourite, when the guy has lost the girl ("Pretty Woman") and the words of the hotel manager, "It must be very difficult to let go of something so beautiful," and then the aside, "You know, Darryl also drove Miss Vivian home yesterday," finally bring the guy to his senses and make him realise what he wants.

The hare should have won the race. The hare was better equipped, fitter, it was entirely within his capability to win. But he did not. In the story of the hare and the tortoise, the tortoise stands no chance, it's a joke race, and so...

Why does the tortoise work so hard? Why does he never quit? Why doesn't he just take a rest?

Look at your dream. Have you ever been told it's impossible? Have you ever been unsure of whether you could achieve it?

Most Zumba Instructors, when I began, were small, lithe Hispanic ladies. I am none of those things. Did I feel like an imposter at the London 2012 Conference? Absolutely. I had already been teaching for over a year, but I felt completely out of place. I wore the gear, I booked the hotel, and I was completely blanked by the other girls in Zumba gear at the hotel at breakfast.

I felt like I did as a teenager at school, that someone somewhere had forgotten to give me the manual, and I did not know how to BE a Zumba Instructor.

Later, after I had been to Zumba Convention, when I learned that I had been "a real boy" all along, I would tell anyone who was heading off to a big gathering, "Say hello, be friendly, and if someone blanks you, then they're not a real Zumba Instructor," because that is not how we roll.

Don't get me started on meditation classes and dismissive yoga teachers.

One of the pieces about Imposter Syndrome I read was about the Cosmopolitan Editor feeling like a huge imposter – because she doesn't always have her nails done, because she doesn't always look put together, because she's not a certain weight. She is not a hare. She does not fit the stereotype of the magazine editor.

Usain Bolt is the wrong shape entirely to be a 100m sprinter – he almost, almost, didn't even try out, because the idea of him being anything other than a 200m or a 400m sprinter was ridiculous. In fact, despite being rather good at winning the fastest race in the world, his heart still belongs to the 200m, and as he says, he wins the 100m for his coach and the 200m for himself.

Some of us need to feel like tortoises in order to do what we want. Our misfit mentality helps us to break new ground, break the rules, learn new ways of doing things, shortcuts and different approaches. (I also learned at London Conference 2012 that Zumba was one of the few places, back then, when being one of the tallest in the room enabled me a great view of the stage – the best since going to see Take That in 1994, when most of the audience were under 13 years old.)

Perhaps Maya Angelou (and I will come back to her story from "I Know Why The Caged Bird Sings") needed to believe that she would never write another book, needed to believe that she would not be read or believed, or taken seriously, in order to write. I spoke in my books before about a cinematic concept called "the wilful suspension of disbelief". It is an extremely valuable concept in theatre, when the audience collectively pretends that the stage is not a stage, that they are sitting watching real events in a real living room (sometimes they also collectively pretend that the play was good too). But sometimes, as artists (and that includes life artists as well as groups of people we often call artists), as dreamers, we have to practise "the wilful suspension of belief". Do you sometimes, as I do, say to yourself as you get ready and rush out of the door, "I'm going to miss the train, I'm going to miss the train"?

Stephen King famously wrote, "Write with the door closed, edit with the door open." Another famous writing practice of his is to write for one person, the "Ideal Reader". Perhaps Maya Angelou, after her experiences at a young age (when she stopped speaking because of the devastating impact of her telling the truth), needed to believe that no one would hear her, no one read her, no one believe her, in order to continue to write.

Maybe, the words of someone close to me when I told them I had written another book, "More books that no one's going to read," while not meant as encouragement, but rather to indicate how foolish my dreams were, acted not just as a negative, but as a spur: unpleasant, chafing, and as a wake up that it was high time I made them eat their own words.

Because, despite the Imposter Syndrome and my own disbelief whenever I see my books being sold, when I heard those words I knew they were unfair, I knew they were untrue and I knew I was going to do something about it.

Sometimes we have to be told we are not, in order to be.

Sometimes we have to be what we are not, in order to be who we are.

Professor McGonagall is not a cat. But she can become a cat. And because she can be a cat, this makes her an excellent witch.

Sometimes we have to let our right hand be ignorant of what our left hand is doing.

And one I personally like, "I am so clever that sometimes I don't understand a single word of what I am saying." Oscar Wilde, The Happy Prince and Other Stories.

Imposter Syndrome as Problem:-

The mask.

Please go and read Don Miguel Ruiz about masks.

We are who we have been trained to be, who we have had to be in order to survive. It is important that we forgive ourselves for what we have had to become in order to get to this point.

Like secret agents we had to put on a mask in order to survive, whether that was at home, at high school, in college, our first jobs, or just around the neighbours. Think of the many, many black people who had to "pass for white" in order to get decent jobs or housing way back when. Think of people who have had to hide their religion or belief system. Think of the Native American people who had to hide their spiritual practices and even "trespass" onto their own land to practise their rites, before these freedoms began to be protected by law.

We have had to become liars.

I forgive myself, and let go of the need to lie.

But it is not easy to put down the mask and to stop pretending to be who we are not.

So sometimes when we walk into the room, feeling like an imposter, it is because we have become so used to acting like another person that our true self feels like the imposter.

Each time we experience that imposter feeling we have to question it; does it serve us, does it go against us, did we need it and do we need it anymore?

Is there any truth when I tell myself that I am not rich enough, not the right class, from the right background or smart enough, pretty enough?

Sometimes our problem is that we are so in denial about the truth that when we seek to be authentic all we can hear is our lies. The voices in our head shout loudly that we are not supposed to be here, doing this, and the mask, the liar in our head, the ego, the person we have created would rather destroy us than allow us to live free.

This is also true in society, of groups of people who have had to pretend to be what they are not in order to survive. Sometimes the most sexist and career blocking person in a business is the woman boss who had to fight so hard to get to where she is. "Why should you have it so easy?"

Sometimes the person who stands in our way is the parent who failed to live their dream. "You will never succeed."

This is not just individual Imposter Syndrome, but inherited, societal.

Do you know the riddle... A man and his son are driving and get into a terrible car crash and they are rushed to hospital. The son needs urgent surgery and is rushed into the operating theatre. The surgeon walks in and says, "I can't operate on this boy. He is my son."

How can this be?

Perhaps you guessed it already, perhaps it took you a moment, but many people have been stumped by this one for far too long. The surgeon is his mother.

The fact that this riddle exists seems ridiculously outdated, and yet, assumptions are still made over and over again that the woman in the scrubs is a nurse.

One of the most powerful things my mother ever said to me was that I could do anything I set my mind to.

Let's all set our minds to overcoming fear of success, because it benefits all of us.

Imposter Syndrome as Origin:-

Cinderella. The daughter of the nobleman made to hide as the kitchen maid, who then pretends to be a noble lady, and who is then found out to be really what she was.

OK, let's take away the noble birth part, because that's really out of date (or should be).

I'm not the pretty one – those are my sisters (this is actually true). I am the fat, tall one, (seriously I am AVERAGE weight and height, how did I buy into this myth), with the horribly lanky hair, who really ought to get a perm (this was the 80s), until the ball where I put on a suit (really, I wore a suit to my first ball) and had an updo. I was beautiful. And two boys fell in love with me. And I started to believe that I could be beautiful.

In the words of that teenage rom com starring Drew Barrymore, "I'm not Josie Grossie anymore."

Most of us grew up with a small group of people, our family, our family friends, school, and once they had decided who we were and what we could be… the brain, the athlete, the beauty, the scientist, the artist… it was very hard to break out of that mould.

I always felt New York was very angry, I think it was the energy of everyone who ran away from home to be who they felt they truly were, and not who they were or were able to be in their home town.

Because of my brother's stroke we had to leave our home town and go somewhere new. At sixteen I was devastated and didn't want to go, but the freedom of walking into a new college and being whoever I wanted to be was life changing. I became beautiful, I had friends, I was not the top of the class for once, I fit in, and I learned that I could relax, I could hang, I could even work hard and compete with others and it didn't matter who came first, second or third – we could laugh about it. There was room at the top.

But I also learned that if I wanted an "A" in English Literature I had to repeat back to the teachers what they wanted to hear about the books we were reading. I had way more freedom in Maths to tell the truth – so that's where I went.

This is not a traditional self help book, so there are no exercises or space for journaling, but I would encourage you to take a moment and examine your "Cinderella" myths. What part of that mould no longer serves you – do you always have to be the responsible one? Do you need to break free of that in order to achieve new dreams? Do you have to accept love from your family as the weak one, the sickly one, the unsuccessful one?

I remember talking to a group of people at The Best You Expo and, I hope this isn't sexist, but we were talking about the "Friends" episode when Monica says to Ross (her brother in case you forgot) something like, "If we could pick our parents, I'd choose yours." None of us have the same parents as our brothers and sisters. (I don't have the same family from day to day, it seems.) And so much of the way we treat each other is bound up in our familial myths, the way our parents were taught. There's another beautiful episode of "Friends" when Monica's grandma dies, and her mother starts to talk about all the ways she was treated growing up, all the put downs and then there's a reflex put down of her own daughter, and look of understanding with Monica and a moment of realisation about what she does to her. It's a start.

Humility

Humility has to be real. Fake humility is just gross.

Success without humility is impossible. That is hubris.

Humility is understanding, as a top transplant surgeon, that your work is useless without the hard work of the person who cleans the operating theatre, let alone the rest of the team.

Humility is understanding that when people are talking about travel and where they'd like to go, that I don't need to share the whole long list of countries I've been to. I don't need to rub it in anyone's face.

Humility is understanding that there is no such thing as independent travel... Did you build the plane? Did you fly it?

No one, not even Jesus, could do it alone.

I write and do many things for myself, but I do not make it happen. I did not create the MacBook, or the language, or the Kindle...

Humility is understanding that while we might be lauded for doing something well, or fast or better than anyone else on the planet, there are millions of others who for some strange societal reason are not honoured for being fantastic at what they do – the people who tend to our loved ones as they are dying or struggling to live, the people who bake our daily bread, the plumbers who make sure our toilets flush... well, you get it.

We are nothing without each other.

And perhaps, just to get political for a second, our world would get along a little better if our politicians remembered that they are public servants, serving not just, in some case, and in some way, the monarch of a country, but every single person who voted for them – and, guess what, every single person who didn't as well.

Service is a word that is used and even misused (I could write another book on "service" as it relates to the jobs that used to exist within English country houses, most of which were described as being "in service"), but we all serve – one way or another.

If we choose to serve money it is easy for us to think we are better than others who have less.

If we serve fame then it's easy to look down on others who have less followers, friends or fans than us.

But if we can serve life, serve what made us who and what we are, if we can serve our dreams without seeking for proof or answers – just trusting the intuition that guides us on our way, we can honour every step – from the times we have to work in a minimum wage job to learn one lesson, to the times when we are ill and unable to work, to the times when we get passed over because it's not our turn or our job, to the time when the most important thing in our world is to stand up and be counted, to stand up and use our voice, our experience and anything else life has given us. With humility we do not have to prove anything to anyone, we don't have to sell, we can just serve, we can just go to the front of the class and teach, we can take the helm, we can do CPR, we can step forward into our own success, our own destiny, because it's what we've been training for this whole time.

Timing is everything.

.

Jealousy as Solution

Say what?

Yes, something I actually love saying to friends and colleagues openly and honestly is, "I'm so jealous."

How could I?

Because if I can recognise the jealousy in me, I can examine it. I can be honest with myself, most importantly.

I'm going to talk about competition too, and I have seen, so many times, the positive side of competition. Competitions and contests have been around for probably as long as we have – in fact I'm pretty sure animals compete too, and so there are great natural benefits from healthy competition.

At its simplest form jealousy says, "I want that."

I'm busy in my work and I feel that is my priority and then someone tells me they are getting engaged. "I want that."

"Do I?"

A part of me that has been sleeping awakes and says, "I want that."

Or, I am feeling societal pressure and I say, "I want that."

Do I really?

Is our jealousy real, do we really want that? Or do we want to be included, do we want some sort of validation?

Is our jealousy reminding us of some part of ourselves we have neglected and we want to embrace now? What part? The part where someone got the promotion or the job, or the next step in our own career?

Another more insidious voice of jealousy is, "I could do that."

Could I?

This can be a great way of getting us on our path, when we see that yes, it is possible for me too to do this.

Or it can be a lie, a way of putting down someone else, someone who is naturally gifted or who works really hard, a way of pulling them down to our level.

I often think this when I watch "Strictly Come Dancing" (the UK version of "Dancing With The Stars"), unfortunately it's probably not true. But I could put on a sexy dress, I could dance with a partner, I could learn some new moves, I could maybe, if I found the right partner, get to do a lift, like Baby in "Dirty Dancing".

In either case how can we handle our jealousy healthily?

By recognising that perhaps we have slipped, that perhaps we want to be more like someone else. Perhaps even that we are being negative about someone because secretly we want to be more like them, yet we are afraid to be.

Perhaps we just want to see if the grass is really greener on the other side? (Maybe we could ask our friends – "What's it really like?" Because that baby, that partner, that job, that career can look great on Instagram, but you might think differently if you heard the full story.)

Perhaps some of our stuff is real, perhaps our lives would have been different if we had been born in a different country, to different parents, had different gifts, but I think if we keep going, if we keep following our path, instead of giving up and just sitting on the sidelines watching other people continue their journeys, then we will come to a place where we can just be grateful for every step, every single second that has brought us to where we are and made us who we were meant to be.

Challenging fear of success is a grief process

Challenging fear of success is a grief process, and it's easy to get stuck.

Grieving is a natural and, I believe, often beautiful process of letting go. Sometimes it's letting go of what is past, sometimes what may never be, and sometimes what exists right now, but that will be lost when your life changes.

It's okay and it's okay to grieve for things and people that others might not understand.

If you think of The Beatles, when was their heyday? Was it when Paul and John played together as teenagers, was it when they experimented with the line up in Liverpool and clubs in Germany, was it those first gigs or the shy young men appearing on American TV for the first time? Was it the enormous stadiums and security that had them thrown in the back of armoured cars? When did their success become a problem rather than a joy?

I remember a story about how they would drive for hours to and from gigs in a van with no heating and they had to create a "Beatle sandwich" where they literally lay on top of each other in the back of the van to keep warm. Of course they probably wouldn't have wanted to go back to those times, but there was a humour and a togetherness that's hard to recreate when everything is going well.

There's a reason that soldiers get together and retell their war stories.

We may be glad "War Is Over" but there is also beauty in the struggle, in the journey that we look back on with fondness.

Success changes our lives, and we are constantly changing, and to be the person we are growing into, we have to let go.

The caterpillar does not necessarily want to become the butterfly, even as it sits and watches others break out in beautiful colours and disappear, because it means letting go of the person we know, the person our friends and family know, and so much of our everyday life.

What I know of grief, and life, and the way I have come to deal with it, is to embrace each step, fully inhabit and love each moment, even as we cry and grieve, enjoy the cheap sandwiches and the good in the struggle, because then we can feel when it no longer serves us, and move on.

That and faith, that if we have the strength to let go we will find more than we have lost... more love, more abundance, more closeness with the people we love. If not, if we hold ourselves back for others, we may end up resenting them, as one day we watch them fly away from us.

Suck the marrow out of life, and then although there may be pain when we move on, there will be less regret.

Bargaining (another part of the grief process)

What would you do if you had a million pounds? What would you do if you had all the time and money in the world?

"I'd give lots to my friends and family and also to charity."

But what would you do for yourself?

"I'd buy a house and go on holiday."

But really, if you could do anything what would you do?

"Oh I don't know, stop bothering me."

One thing I know is that the universe provides. This year money has been tight, and I've been through many phases when I've been poor, and I've learned a lot from those times. This year I would have been happy to get a job packing boxes in a warehouse for minimum wage. This year I lived with a lady with dementia because it was a job and a roof over my head. I did other things because I was poor, and boy did I learn a lot. But mostly I gave. I gave my time, I gave my love, I gave my compassion, and I bit my tongue when, quite honestly, if I'd had more money I'd have walked out the door. But really, the lack of money was only part of it, because in moments of clarity I knew I was doing God's work, I knew I was on another part of my apprenticeship, I knew I was being trained and I was serving where I was being called to serve.

At the end of each phase I reached another milestone with money. That's how I knew I had arrived. The money was significant, but not important. It signified that it was time to move on.

"I don't have the time and the money." The two biggest excuses we use today (I am sure in the past it was social convention, and money). A few weeks ago, as things were getting better financially, I wrote a few promises to myself. "As soon as I have the money I am going to do... this... and this... and this... and this..."

And the money arrived. Don't get me wrong, I don't think that just writing those promises made the money arrive. But there's a whole process of getting ready for something, for the next phase, like leaving college, and I could start to see that light, and so I started planning, and perhaps the universe allowed the money to arrive a little bit earlier, because it knew I was going to keep my promises, and not just forget, not just get that cash, that time, and go and spend it on socks.

Time and time again the universe delivers what we need. I have discovered so many times, when I didn't have the money, that I could get what I needed for free, I could do it DIY, on the cheap, in fact people would pay me for it. Yes, I got paid to live in my dream house, but as it was with a lady with dementia... (The truth is that I had some incredible moments of perfect bliss, helping her, and I learned like crazy.

Including the rather terrifying truth that yes, Marmite does eventually go mouldy.) But... we say, "I'd do this if I could afford it. I'd do this if I had the time..." It arrives and then we squander it.

So is this bargaining? It's certainly throwing away success over and over again, because we tell ourselves we just don't have the wherewithal.

I decided a long time ago to stop telling myself, "I don't have the time, I don't have the money..." and see what happened. A lot of good things, and also times when I really didn't have the cash. And guess what, when I really didn't have the money to do something, I found a reason a little while down the road, and there were moments when I just couldn't bring myself to spend so much money... until that time in Hawai'i when the only place available cost nearly $500 a night. Yes, the universe works in mysterious ways.

Origins

Black Magic

Am I seriously writing a chapter called "Black Magic"?
Yes.

Before you freak out, listen for thirty seconds. I am using this term specifically as taught by Don Miguel Ruiz, whose four agreements begin with "Be Impeccable With Your Word". Black magic is what happens when we use the word against ourselves.

Most of the time we do it unconsciously. We have absorbed or been taught some lie that we perpetuate, we keep some punishment alive by re-enacting it over and over and over again on ourselves. We believe the lie that something bad happened and we deserved it, or we caused it. We believe the lie that we are incapable or stupid or ugly.

We believe that we do not deserve good things.

We believe "good things" are what other people say they are, not what feels good to us.

We believe that we have to marry someone rich to support us.

We believe we cannot leave an abusive relationship.

We believe we cause or deserve the abuse.

We believe we have to support all the people around us.

We believe lies, consciously or unconsciously.

In my books, the "Camino de la Luna" series, I wrote in detail about all the boundaries and barriers, all the lies I had learned to believe, and each situation I was in forced me to relearn what the world is, how it works, who I am. I believe that sometimes we have to strike out on a wing and a prayer to the other side of the world to learn and undo the curses we have unwittingly picked up (like viruses) in our lives, and sometimes all we need to do is to sit and watch a Christmas movie.

When you follow your heart and aim for success (even if it turns out to not really be what you want) you are doing the work of unravelling the lies, the curses and the black magic in your life.

The truth will set you free.

It's too easy

Lydia Grant (Debbie Allen's character) in "Fame": "You've got big dreams. You want fame. ... Well fame costs, and right here is where you start paying; in sweat."

Who doesn't love "Fame"?
Leave the room.

But as much as I love it (and yes, of course, I've had years of paying in sweat, learning to be a half decent Zumba Instructor), I'll tell you what happened when I trained, and sweat, and did all the video trainings, and live trainings and masterclasses and then took a break and then trained to peak fitness and put together the most amazing, perfect Zumba Gold® class anyone had ever seen.

I freaked out my one student. She couldn't keep up, couldn't do one tenth, one twentieth, one tiny bit of it. One of those steps, one or two of those routines would have been enough. I would have been enough of a teacher for her before my first Zumba class, with what I knew naturally and did dancing around my bedroom when I was eleven.

But I would never have believed that something which was so natural; dancing around and having a little sweat – doing the moves that felt good and natural to me would ever be of any use to anyone else. And, in fairness, she wouldn't have been able to keep up with me then either.

What Zumba really taught me (as well as all the "more") was how to do less. How to lead so that people could follow:-

- Three steps, more or less to each track
- Repeat the same bit of choreography to the same bit of music (a tried and tested method in dance and dance aerobics, before Zumba)
- Simplify if your class cannot keep up – for example, just do the arms or the legs
- Slow down if the class can't keep up, to half speed, or even quarter speed
- If it's a real disaster, go back to the drawing board or ditch the track for the next class
- Don't be afraid to repeat the same song, two or three times if the class really struggle
- If it's too difficult for them at all, give them water breaks, instead of teaching straight through (as you'd do for a master class)
- If all else fails, abandon Zumba (where we never break down) and just break the damn thing down. But try to keep the music going and keep the vibe going.

Did I do any of this when my one poor student was struggling in this particular class? No I did not. Because I knew I was teaching the right way, and I knew that when I taught regular classes, slowing down for that one student did not serve them because it made them feel singled out, and pissed the rest of the class off – instead they got to be congratulated for having done so well by the rest of the class, and given tips and camaraderie, "Oh yes, that step is really rough – it took me ages, let me show you how I managed it". It wasn't hazing but you can see how it brought them into the class – it made them one of us.

But I didn't have the rest of my class – what I was doing didn't work, the way I was doing it was wrong – but I carried on, because my ego kept telling me I was right and my student was wrong. Which made me wrong, (or an arse, if you prefer).

It's hard for us to believe that the best way is the simplest way. That sometimes the most we have to offer is the least we can deliver. Susan Jeffers said this too, about her first "Feel the Fear" class – she walked in with pages of notes, enough for a whole series of classes, but luckily she only tried to deliver the warm up, the introduction, the first step.

How can what I do so easily, so naturally, so quickly, be of any use, interest or value to anyone else?

How can it be that sometimes even what I deliver, what I sell to others is actually nothing?
(This is when it gets Zen.)

Not smoking, not eating, not shopping, not getting angry, not speaking, not exercising, throwing away your possessions, understanding that less is more, deleting the needless words in a person's manuscript… Just being present while someone does their own work, or even while they are sleeping. How can nothing, or less than nothing be so valuable?

How can Zen masters make a living from teaching how to stop thinking?

The Gladiator – I Am Spartacus

In the Roman arena it was simple. One lives, one dies. I succeed, you die. I cannot survive, I cannot triumph without causing another's demise.

In my book "Camino de la Luna – Unconditional Love" I talked about confronting the dreadful fears that came up as I tried to go to Hawai'i. Deep in my being I had ingested the idea that whenever I left my family, something bad happened - rooted in the death of my grandfather when I moved to Paris. If I look further back I see that my other grandfather passed away when my siblings and I had to stay with my other grandparents because of family illness. Somehow I made it my fault, and the answer was never to stray too far, never to fly too high.

When I was in Rome working on this book, a little voice kept whispering in my head, "You're going to kill someone."

Eh?

So I just listened and tried to figure out what this little voice was trying to say.

At about the same time as my brother suffered a stroke, I won my first writing award outside of school. I got a second prize (in two categories!) Can you think how bad it would have been if I had won first prize?

Yes, my ego had made it all about me. I win, you lose. I succeed, you die.

My fear of success married my survivor guilt, and lived happily ever after. My words, my writing, became secretive, sneaky; reviews, poetry, screenplays, articles, a website…

This is not an origin for everyone, and yet, how many of us can truly celebrate or enjoy our success openly and without censure from others. Don't get too happy, says society, or the other shoe will drop.

That little voice inside me said, "Don't do it. Don't write your book. Don't publish your books whole-heartedly. Don't go all out. Because if you win, someone will die. And it will be your fault."

I win, you lose.

I succeed, someone out there dies.

It is not true. And the best way to silence that lying voice in your head is to listen, to unravel, to hold it up to the light and it becomes so clear what a liar it is.

And it disappears.

When I look at the Zumba organisation I see how something great has come from one person's dreams and desires. I see how many people can be helped by one person. His success has saved lives, maybe even my life. Not because he did it all. He had help. He had an army.

Kinda like Spartacus.

The problem is that this kind of thinking is subtle, it is ingrained, and so it can be as much of a societal problem as an individual one. Our parents may also worry when we succeed, and it can be a fine line between a fear of our flying too high, like Icarus, and jealousy.

Our teachers, our parents want to teach us to do the right thing, and so, when their thinking gets twisted around, what happens is that we get the message – winning is wrong, or perhaps, we shouldn't spend so long focusing on one thing, perhaps we shouldn't show off, perhaps we should let someone else take centre stage. Perhaps we should be more of a team player, let someone else play, let someone else win for once.

Disapproval, resentment – these can sometimes be the result of our succeeding. Sometimes our success results in punishment.

And sometimes it is our peers who punish us, who shun us. Sometimes we scare them. Either they want to maintain the status quo, or they are scared of what might happen if we rock the boat, what might change.

Sometimes our confidence, our abilities can be misunderstood as arrogance or hubris. "You think you're so great!" They want to cut us down to size. They want to make sure we don't get too big for our boots. They want to keep us in line. Sometimes they make fun of us because they believe or want to believe it's for our own good.

And sometimes they don't think that what we are doing is good enough. When I started teaching Zumba several friends told me that I shouldn't. I had two degrees. I was too smart to be a fitness teacher. I was selling myself short. Looking back, I can see that these friends did not have university degrees or a degree in a subject as rigorous as Maths, to them I was throwing that success away for something easy. Whereas my family understood that fitness, wellbeing is everything when you don't have it – they knew it wasn't just about losing weight. They respect keeping fit.

On the other hand, I face more resistance from my family when I write. To my friends this is amazing, that I can write a book. They respect this work.

We are not just healing ourselves when we face down fear of success – we are facing down a disease of the mind. When Spartacus stood up for himself, for another slave in the same situation, for the female slave he had fallen in love with, he was not just fighting his fight. He was changing the world.

I have been the first to do many things, not just the first woman. And I never believed it was an issue. I remember when I was standing to be the first female Film Secretary (manager of the film club) at university and someone asked the question, "How would you handle it if you had to kick someone out of the cinema?"

My answer was simple. I'd ask them to leave. Because male or female, none of us should be getting physical with a customer. (There's also anecdotal evidence that women bouncers are more "successful" than men, because it's rarer for a man being asked to leave a club to get physical with a woman doing the asking.)

I also wasn't strong enough to carry the cans of film by myself. I had to get help.

And once I was voted in, I never really had time to worry about either of these jobs again. I was too busy running the place, being flown to national film festivals and having lunch at BAFTA (and trying not to get kicked off my degree because I'd spent too much time on films).

John Winston Ono Lennon MBE,
9 October 1940 – 8 December 1980

I wrote such a detailed account of my journey from London, all the way around the world and back, to find a part of me I had let go of, the writing part, for too many bad reasons. That account ended in the Spring of 2018. And then I went back to travelling. In the Summer of 2018 I explored England, not least Liverpool.

I wandered around, trying to see Liverpool, I stood next to the amazing statues of the Fab Four on the dock. And then I went in to see an exhibition on the life of John Lennon, curated by Yoko Ono.

John Lennon's story has always been tied up for me with my dad's, he died tragically early too, when he was estranged from us, although he had tentatively reached out in the last year or so of his life. My father was also a musician and an artist. I am sure that there were also many of my dad's fashion and music choices that had a lot to do with the influence of The Beatles and Lennon.

So, that exhibition was about John Lennon, his life, his regrets, and understanding that just before his death, he was finally happy, finally making bread, spending time with his baby son and reaching out to his older son, this was the John Lennon of "Beautiful Boy (Darling Boy)", but of course it opened up emotions for me, and I stood there and looked at his poor broken glasses and cried and cried and cried. And then went across the road to the Youth Hostel and cried and cried and cried some more.

Success for many of us involves exposure. The painting has to be shown, the movie, the book has to be released, even if no one comes to the show.

We are sharing a gift. But not everyone is going to love that gift. For some of us the reaction will be polarised, and we won't know whether to be more scared of the desperate fans who love us, or the critics who hate us.

Today, more than ever, the artist is exposed. Not just to the professional critics, but to the internet noise, to the single individual who misreads the book, who criticises not just what was written but also what was not written. And it is one thing to use the power of one of the Four Agreements, "Do not take anything personally," it is one thing to deal with jealousy, even from friends and family, even censure, anger, disgust at what we have chosen to create, but it is another for a writer or an artist to have to go into hiding from death threats.

We remember John Lennon.

And so, in the end, in writing this book, I have to ask how we can hold this fear, our fear that success may bring us the very worst that society can offer, as well as all the good things.

John Lennon sang, "The monster's gone."

Yoko Ono sang on "Beautiful Boys," "Don't be afraid to be afraid..."

And then, as I woke up this morning, I understood. Because I had been thinking about my dear friend/ex-lover who died in a mountaineering accident, and about other people who have died in tragic circumstances. My travelling and adventuring has taught me not to be afraid, but to be wise, to consider carefully what resources I need for any outing, even if it is just a walk in the park. To understand how to check and plan for problems, but also to know that there may always be a force majeure, a snowstorm, a rock fall, an unexpected financial hit, we were not born to be safe, but to explore.

We cannot protect from any eventuality, we cannot hide from freak accidents or people with severe mental health problems.

But we can do what we love, and if we have to go, we can die doing what we love.

John Lennon died doing what he loved. It's the only comfort I have when I think about my friend who died in the mountains. That, and knowing how many amazing adventures he had already had in the mountains, on the water, in the snow, in the jungle, that he had met so many people, that he had inspired so many.

"They shall not grow old." I will always now be older than my father ever was, than John Lennon, than my friend.

We can't hide under the bed forever and be happy.

I'm not talking about being a hero, I'm not talking about self-sacrifice, I'm talking about a much maligned and misunderstood term used by psychologist Abraham Maslow – self-actualisation. In his own words this is what it means:-

"What a man can be, he must be."

"A musician must make music, an artist must paint, a poet must write, if he is to be ultimately happy."

"The desire to become more and more what one is, to become everything that one is capable of becoming."

In the Summer of 2018 I also "flew" with the dolphins in Madeira. I lay on the net of a catamaran as we soared over the water, pods of wild dolphins playing with their babies underneath the net. This is freedom, this is self-actualisation, for me and for them; a stark contrast to visiting captive dolphins in Mexico circling around and around a tiny, noisy pool in the centre of an apartment complex, where all I could do was silently communicate with them the joy of playing in the waves.

We cannot let the fear of the vast, beautiful, living ocean, no matter what monsters may lie in the deep, keep us in a concrete tank.

Speaking Truth to Power

When I read "The Book of Joy", I heard a great expression "speaking truth to power" - it's something that Archbishop Desmond Tutu did a lot during the days of apartheid in South Africa and which he continues to do today, whether it is calling out the South African government for refusing to give the Dalai Lama permission to visit him, because of political pressure from the Chinese government, or whether it is calling out fellow Nobel Peace Prize winner Aung San Suu Kyi for standing by in the face of what appears to be ethnic cleansing (what a phrase – don't we mean another holocaust?) It is the act of using our words, using the power of speech to say what is true, regardless of how big or scary or demonic or powerful the person, the body, the government, the movement is that we are calling out. It's a little bit more than complaining or writing a letter to the papers (which can also be a powerful act).

I am so proud to witness moments like this, moments when the little guy stands up and says, "No". It's too easy to remain silent, it's too easy to let it be. There is nothing spiritual about watching abuse and ignoring it.

I am reminded of the people who tried to speak up, speak out about Lance Armstrong, who were silenced, discredited, slurred, shut out... and the ones who tried to protect him, protect their sport, and the ones who sat on the fence until the tide turned.

I am talking about the ones who could not speak truth to power. I am talking about the ones who did not have the strength, the maturity or the know how to even begin to speak about what they knew.

It is famously written and quoted that we are more scared of our power, of our light than our dark, but here is something else: I think that many of us are ashamed of our power.

Because we were not always powerful. We were all small once, we have all been scared, of something real or unreal, usually both, we have all had to hide or run.

We have all had moments when our ego shouted, "Freeze!"

And in those moments, often, our soul too called out, "Freeze!"

"Do nothing, be quiet and silent and still."

I wish I could forgive myself for those moments. And yet I understand why I could not, can never forgive.

Because there is nothing to forgive.

There are moments when we are powerless, or to act, to speak would be worse than to stay silent.

(And, of course, there are moments when we should act and speak, no matter how powerful the obstacle appears.)

#MeToo is not a movement I have a great deal of understanding of, but at the same time I understand completely. One person speaks, and then another, and another. One person acts, then another and another.

The other day, a friend told me a secret she had been carrying for years, and I told her a secret I had been carrying for a year. It wasn't really a secret, but something I wouldn't have told her, because I didn't want to hurt her. I didn't think she would understand. And when we spoke, a little light crept into the dark. My burden became a little lighter, because it was less of a secret, and we could both say to each other, "You shouldn't have had to go through that."

So let me try to use my words, let me try to speak truth to power, to you, in this book. If, like me, there are moments when something extraordinarily good happens, and then there is a little negative reaction, when you don't feel that you deserve something, when you wait, like the Gladiator for another to be put to death for your success, hear this:-

It's not your fault, it's not your fault, it's not your fault. You were too small, too weak, too ignorant, too poor, too penniless, too confused to be able to help, no matter how much you wanted to, no matter how much it tortured you. You were unable to find the right words, the right actions that would have helped the situation. You did your best. You did your best. You did your best. If you stayed small, if you stayed silent, if you *let things happen*, it was not your choice, it was survival, and you chose life, you chose to listen to your heart and maybe you chose to hide in the shadows, maybe you let others suffer, maybe, maybe…

But that was then and this is now. Now you can make a choice, now you can speak, now you can take action, now you can use your power, now you can use your voice, your strength, now you are a force of nature, now when you choose life you choose extraordinary, earth shaking, heaven shifting, life changing, feet moving, body thrilling… stuff.

It is not your fault that there were moments in your life when you could not be you, when you could not find the words, when you could not take the action. Do not be ashamed. Do not believe the lie that you could have done better – you did… your best. You did your best. You did your best.

Do not let what you had to do in the past in order to survive hold you back now. I want you to go out there now and do your best today, set your own power free, you are not a victim, you are a survivor, so live.

Take One For The Team (and other lies)

Some people, in order to be successful, need to learn to work well with others.

Some people, in order to be successful, need to learn to wander off alone.

What is the drama?

I'll tell you. There's a lot of false success mythology (success crap) that says you need a team. And no one says it louder than the people who want to be in someone else's team because they're scared to wander off alone, or the people who need a team for what they want to do.

What is true? There is no such thing as independent travel. Unless you made your shoes, your rucksack, your water bottle, the plane that flew you there. (I'm not talking about the people who wander off into the woods like Henry David Thoreau – but even he took books, and he did not make them himself.) We are all standing on the shoulders of giants, but in the words of Kahlil Gibran, "Let there be spaces in your togetherness."

There is a time for togetherness and a time for solitude.

I've lost a lot of time in my life to Monday morning meetings, where "managers" do the outdated practice of "decimating" their team. Somebody gets it in the neck, whose turn is it this week? Even something as positive as "Strictly

Come Dancing" (the UK's version of "Dancing With The Stars") has one couple going out each week, it has judges that can be positively cruel. The team dynamic often works in very non-team ways.

Can you imagine trying to write a book with a team? People do it (in fact it's a lot like making a movie), but for me, often writing a book, especially this one, makes me feel like a crazed scientist trying to get all the inspirational thoughts down in a way that makes sense before they disappear again. This is not a team sport, this is a 100m sprint, sometimes for three days. This is wandering in the woods with nothing to show for it for a week. I do not want to have to explain it to anyone. This is me being Einstein, looking at light on the water and understanding everything and nothing simultaneously. This is me being bad tempered when Vodafone rings me and texts me to talk about my plan ("My plan, my plan is you leave me alone at 4:30 in the morning") and not wanting, but needing to be alone. (Ask Shonda Rhimes, who writes beautifully about this in "Year of Yes".)

Usain Bolt describes in his autobiography making the career decision; to focus on either cricket or sprinting. His father tells him – run. In cricket you are only as good as your team, in running you are as good as you can get.

Icarus may have benefitted from being in a team.

There is a huge responsibility to being a leader, whether you are a team leader, or a spiritual leader, a business leader or a charity spokesperson. Sadly many people achieve the notional success of these positions before having achieved the true success of being authentic, of being able to be truthful. So they lie. Perhaps they lie in order to cover up their lack of knowledge, or experience, or perhaps to cover up breaking rules, either because they don't believe in those rules or they don't believe that they can succeed without breaking them.

I read an article this week about a famous liar, one of the most famous. Of all the people who had been cheated and hurt by this person, the one who finally got through to him about what he had done was someone who had worked for him, someone who could finally make him see that when he lied, he didn't just lie, he made all the people in his team into liars. He made so many people, either knowingly or unknowingly, cheats and liars too.

Leaders have a responsibility. Whether it's giving well-researched advice as a fitness professional, especially about nutrition and sports drinks (which the Mayo Clinic has recommended fitness coaches should advise people not to drink) or being honest when canvassing for charity donations or votes about where the money is really going.

If we cannot be good leaders, then we must fall back and let others lead, we must learn better before we put others at risk of the consequences of our decisions.

But it is not just the leader of the team who is important, that's why there's a saying, "You are only as good as your weakest link." It's not always true, but a weak link can destroy a team, especially when it is the team doctor.

Some people like teams because it means they can coast. They don't have to make their own decisions. They can follow. It's easier. But we have to be constantly evaluating our team, and whether it works, even if it's the "team" of family, friends… what a lot of people would call a support network. We may have to move people around or fire them.

Why?

Because you have to know who you can trust. If I get into a taxi cab in a foreign country, if I go on a walk through the rainforest, if I get on a boat, or on a bus, I make a decision. I trust the leader. Or… as sometimes happens, I say, "Hell no," and run in the opposite direction.

Be sceptical but learn to listen.

If your friends jumped off a cliff, would you do it too?

It is too late when you're in the jungle. It is too late when you are on a boat in the middle of the ocean.

It is too late when you are under the knife, under anaesthesia in an operating theatre.

Choose your team wisely.

Choose your doctor most especially wisely (and your cleaner).

Prince, Michael Jackson, Elvis Presley and so many more talented solo performers relied on expertise and advice from people that did not serve them. (Or they chose the people who gave them the advice they wanted – who knows.)

Sometimes you can do it alone (sometimes you have to) and other times you may be part of the Philharmonic. Either way you have to master your own instrument, you have to do your own practice, and if the conductor leads you wrong, if the person in the next row keeps getting the timing wrong, sometimes you have to take action to correct the direction of the team, and sometimes you have to find a new place to play.

Written In The Body

This year I went to a personal development expo in London to help out my friend Hayley Felton. I benefitted not just from the connections I made with others, but also because I was able to talk completely honestly with her about the challenges I'd been facing.

I had nailed it down to a big fear of success, which I'm tackling, and a nasty habit of hiding (something which teaching Zumba helped me to overcome) and I'd progressed from completely freaking out the first time I saw one of my books on the Free Amazon Best-Seller chart to being frustrated that my books weren't higher on the Paid Amazon Best-Seller charts, but I am still awfully good at hiding, when I need to be much better at pearling (i.e. standing out and shining!) Talking about this with Hayley, we decided that I should look at the talks at the expo and find ones that might really help (hanging out with Hayley was also a good start). As we sat on the train after setting up, I read out each talk...

She looked down at the page when I'd finished. "What about this one?" She pointed at a talk about... dun, dun, dun... "Fear of Success." I had literally not seen it. I had looked at and read every single description but had ignored this.

I needed a coach. Luckily Hayley is a great coach. So we decided that I had to head to that talk.

I'd like to share with you what I learned.

The coach, Mas Sajady, actually taught what he called a "medi-healing" which is a combination of meditation and healing and is designed to create immediate results (unlike many of the coaches who were selling an expensive program).

As I sat in the session I went down into all the reasons I hide, and hide my gifts. Some of them are clear to me and so obvious (like when Hayley pointed out the talk in the brochure), and yet... the coach/healer spoke about our heritage, our instincts and our DNA... our family habits as well as our personal habits. I realised that much of the stuff I can talk about so freely now (as can Hayley and this coach) would have got us sentenced to death as witches not so long ago, and locked up in insane asylums even more recently. So many of the things I've learned around the world about healing have had to go underground in order to survive. So the fact that I exist, with my DNA, with my family's heritage of artists, healers, intuitive people, people who stand up and write about things they feel are important, is a miracle.

When I went to Scotland before, I discovered so much about my father's family and how they had to keep going into hiding to avoid the soldiers who wanted to catch them, kill them or even send them to the Southern States of the US as slaves. 12 times they had all their possessions stolen from their land and had to go into hiding near their farm... It is a miracle that I am alive.

But my DNA has survived because, guess what, my family were all such good hiders for generations. And so the penny drops.

I've called what I do being a shaman (maybe a modern shaman) or a wise woman in the tradition of so many of the wise women of England who were sacrificed as witches, and I've felt strongly for years that one of my spirit animals is the leopard. After a very powerful dream in Scotland I looked it up – the leopard is the spirit animal of the shaman. And perhaps this is because, like my family, leopards are extremely good hiders.

So perhaps that's why I am a pearl, because it's time now for who I am and what I do to come out of the shadows. Because, like any spiritual seeker, I am looking for what we all seek; truth, because truth brings freedom and with it finally, peace.

Hide Like A Leopard

(written after the hottest day recorded – July 2019)

This phrase has been going around my head since last week, and it was never more appropriate than yesterday in the heat, where the only thing for me to do was to lie down in the shade, in the woods and drink lots of water. Sometimes hiding out is the wisest thing we can do.

But the week before I was thinking of my decision in South Africa, when I realised how much I had been afraid to stand out and be seen, the decision of "No More Hiding". And yet, I've been hiding a lot, in one of my new roles as a carer, and I've been doing it extremely well - except instead of hiding up in a tree I'm hiding up in a room to stay out of the way of other carers when they're on duty. It's a bit like a story I heard of a man who worked from home, but every day pretended to leave and go to work so that his children wouldn't follow him to his study.

All of these different concepts rolled into my head - the hiding that we do out of fear of success, the hiding we do behind others, the hiding our work so that we don't get judged, the hiding by not doing it at all, but, as I wandered around getting supplies the day before the real heat hit, it struck me that perhaps instead of "hiding like a mouse" as I was thinking of earlier times, if I look at my actions and honour everything that was going on, for me and in the world around me, I was really always "hiding like a leopard".

As we confront any fear of success there is a price to pay, even if it's just the energy cost of the shaking knees and the sweaty palms. It takes it out of us, so, just as with fitness, we don't suddenly, overnight go from the Before to the After picture, it takes work, and one step at a time. We are going as fast as we can.

So, while we need to use everything around us to move forward, inspiration from others, sometimes even the lows of escaping a certain uncomfortable situation, we also need to have patience and compassion with ourselves. We are always hiding like a leopard, and we will always pounce at the perfect moment.

And, of course, there is another meaning to this phrase - that beautiful skin coveted by so many, especially poachers. I do not want to spread fear, just wisdom, but as I've learned from travelling - despite loving the world and wanting to serve the world, I don't walk around with my purse or my rucksack wide open. We also need to honour our gifts, and treat ourselves and what we have to offer with respect. (And respect those who don't want to be taught by us - or see our beautiful hide!)

Some people will always try to take advantage, and so, perhaps one of the reasons we hide, I hide, they hide, is to allow enough personal growth so that when we do come out into the open in order to perhaps, sell a product or a service, that we do so with respect and honour on both sides - after all, every interaction we have with another is a sacred thing and it is important that our exchange of money or energy honours both sides.

We do not serve people fully when we allow them to take advantage of us.

The Competition

There's a great moment in "Grey's Anatomy" when a musician (having brain surgery, aren't they always) says about losing his friends when he started to get the gigs they all wanted, "That's when I realised, they weren't my friends, they were the competition."

What I love about book people (authors and publishers and book sellers) is that, aside from the rejection letters and endless negativity that comes with submissions, they genuinely want each other to succeed. Yes, it would be nice to be at the top of the charts, but like musicians and filmmakers there's a vibe here – we know that we are constantly making a bigger pie. Nobody says, "Oh I read a good book last week, I don't need to read another one." The Oscars get everyone excited about going to the cinema (even if they're going to see a blockbuster that would NEVER feature in the Oscars). The run down of the charts on the radio gets everyone listening to new tracks.

There's no party without everyone else.

Great athletes may want to "annihilate the competition," but they also want to race against, compete against the best.

One of my favourite movies of all time is "The Big Blue". Enzo, one of the main characters, is the world champion free diver. The first thing that he does (apart from doing up the car), when he gets a windfall, is to track down the boy he used to compete with when he was a kid. He knows that he is not the world champion unless he competes against "The Frenchman". They compete, they have fun, they laugh at the other competitors, because they are brothers. No one else in the world can understand who they are and what they do, it's like they share the same skin, no one else can understand the way it feels.

I loved my Zumba Christmas parties. I loved offering a stupid, worthless prize for a competition, usually to do a move that my class had struggled with all year. It never failed to surprise me that, in a few moments, every person in the room, competing with each other, did better than they had all year. They rocked it. Why did they need that competition?

Perhaps it is our animal nature? Perhaps, when there is one mate to win, one piece of food, one place to rest, we rise and we get a little extra something from somewhere that we never knew we had.

Competition can be healthy and joyous, or it can be bitter and hurtful.

Sibling rivalry can be an example of the best and the worst (remember Cain and Abel?)

In the movie "A League of Their Own", the two sisters fight over who is the best, they argue and act like little kids.

Finally one walks away, and the scrapper, the one who fought so hard, says something along the lines of, "I never wanted you to quit."

Sometimes it's hard to tell.

All other teachers are wrong (trust me)

I'm kidding. But it's very important, if you are going to face your fear of success, that you understand what Don Miguel Ruiz called "The Fifth Agreement" (and yes, there's an awfully good book about it) – "Be sceptical but learn to listen".

All fitness teachers are wrong.

They are wrong for somebody (and that somebody might be you). Just because they teach for anyone and everyone who wants to take their class, does not mean that it's right for you. You are unique and wonderful and your body may be different, or your way of working may be different. They may be right and wonderful for someone else – but it may not be you.

I cannot really do yoga. It's wrong for my body type, because I'm hyper flexible. I do yoga every morning (pretty much) but it is just a few specific moves rolled in with some physio prescribed exercises for my back.

I can't do squats – well, one type of squat. It's wrong for my back and the challenges I have. The other type of squat is great for me.

I try to be vegan, I eat a lot of vegan food. But I can't eat a lot of mushroom based food – it makes me ill.

Every teacher is wrong for someone. So before your ego gets involved and tells you you have to meditate for four hours, or go to Bali and learn how to be an Ashtanga yoga teacher, before you try to follow someone's else path, remember *your* success is different to anyone else's.

It's okay to be a practising vegan who wears a leather jacket (me), or who eats the meat off a friend's plate before it goes in the bin (me), who cooks meat for their family.

It's okay to be a yogi who doesn't do yoga (me).

It's okay to be a meditation teacher who is wary of meditating.

Meredith Grey from "Grey's Anatomy": "My mother used to say this about residency, 'It takes a year to learn how to cut. It takes a lifetime to learn not to.' Of all of the tools on the surgical tray, sound judgment is the trickiest one to master."

All teachers, all spiritual practices are wrong for someone, and it might just be you. One man's meat is another man's poison.

Do not let your ego abuse you by lying, by telling you that your success is being, doing or having something that is not right for you.

And even if you practice one thing for years, you must remember, as a Buddhist might say, "Do not confuse the raft with the shore." The purpose of meditation is not to get good at meditation. The purpose of yoga is not to get good at yoga.

The purpose of all these things is to equip you with what you need to live your life to the fullest – to be successful, whatever that authentic success is for you.

In the words of Krishnamurti, "The truth is a pathless land."

Even the path that saved us before will not be there when we turn around. We know the river is always changing, "You cannot step into the same river twice," but so is the dust and the dirt under our feet, so is the sand – you can never walk along the same beach twice. You are not the same person two days in a row, you have already changed, transformed. On my Camino I said so often, of not planning, not booking a hotel, "I don't know who I'm going to be tomorrow."

Five year plan. Don't make me laugh.

Can you really self-sabotage?

I believe that every time you have "self-sabotaged" in the past it was the right thing for you, because it got you to this moment. But what if it's enough now, what if it's time to stop, because you don't need it anymore.

That's why you're here - you specifically and me specifically.

Whether it was a book or a class I have never had anyone walk in who was not meant to be there, even if it was in order to say, "This is not for me." Every breath you take is on purpose. You, are on purpose.

So you couldn't manifest a million pounds. You weren't supposed to. Whether that was because you were supposed to get off your arse and invent something or create something, or work for someone, or sell something... it was all working FOR you, happening FOR you, not TO you.

I work in the dark, in ignorance, because if I could have seen what the last few years would bring me I would have been too happy to wait and too sad to let go. But my lack in that time took me exactly where I was supposed to be and allowed me to stay for exactly the perfect amount of time. It was all happening perfectly, even if I only had enough faith, or enough money, or enough food, or enough shelter or enough anything for one more day. Sometimes, just having enough for one more hour, one more minute is all it takes to get us through, and NOT having serves us just as much as having TOO MUCH. (You learn this when you carry a rucksack as much as I have, or when you try to fly cabin bag only on EasyJet.)

So I failed to manifest a million pounds, or a perfect body, or my perfect relationship. Because those things would just have got in the way. And also because, sitting in one spot trying to manifest something would be like Howard Hughes sitting in a hotel room demanding everything be brought to him - honestly not that much fun.

The universe is wiser than us. (And, if you believe just that one sentence, think how much at odds it is with so many people, so many spiritual teachers who tell you just to do it with your thinking.)

If I want a cup of tea, I will almost always have to get up and make it myself. And I would much rather that, I would rather have legs that stand and can walk me to the kitchen, arms strong enough to lift a kettle, the sense to know how to do it, the ability to be able to drink, and all that, than to have to sit and wait for someone to bring it to me. I would rather wipe my own arse, thank you very much.

Doing Your Best

Don't worry, I'm not going to go all cheap motivational speaker on you and tell you that you only live once.

I'm going to say, you did your best, we always do, we do our best to keep our hearts open to others, we do our best, and we do suffer the pain of loss and letting go, so if you can be awake to this truth you need never feel regret. You did your best. There is no need to regret.

Just remember that if you focus your energy on staying open, on loving unconditionally it may take everything you have, but please, please don't regret that either. It is an act of heroism. To love when there is no hope is pure heroism. (Or foolishness according to others.) At some point here, someone might say that this is what differentiates us from the animals. They obviously never met my dog.

Just try one more time.

How do you survive success?

I would not be honest in writing this book if I did not talk honestly about suicide.

If this touches you please remember, this is just a book, it is not a helpline, it is not a therapist or a doctor, it is not a friend, or a hug. If this touches, reach out for help. In the darkness, when things become confused, suicide can seem like an answer. It is not.

Let's talk about surviving.

If anything ever whispers that you would be better off dead, it is lying to you.

If anything every whispers that people would be better off without you, it is lying to you.

I wish that we didn't have to have this conversation, but if you picked up this book, the chances are that you have dreams and goals that you are struggling with, and that can be for all sorts of reasons. Some of the reasons, our origins and our origin stories can be more challenging, more dark and twisty than others. Sometimes it feels as though we cannot go on. Please take a breath. And then another. And another.

I was reading a book by a famous cancer survivor who talked about the dark time AFTER he was cured. That was when everything hit, all the emotions and the pain and so many emotions from the treatment, and worse, the waiting… for each test, for each scan, to see if it would come back.

I've been through some pretty bad waiting, and it can feel impossible.

Sometimes we feel as though we don't deserve life. We don't deserve the great things falling into our laps. We don't deserve love and joy.

Certainly we do not deserve more than many other people who have been dealt a harder hand than us. But I believe we can find ways to embrace our good fortune without acting as though we believe we deserve it more than others. We don't have to be dicks about it. (That's where the humility kicks in.)

Life is good.

Enjoy life.

Remember you are alive, every day.

It is hard to allow the emotions, to feel real emotions everyday. It can feel like death, because it is death of the ego, it is a grief process, it is saying goodbye to one life and hello to a new one.

It is a miracle, because so few people manage it in this lifetime, to actually be alive, instead of sleepwalking through it.

There is an idea that I love which goes something like this – "At our death we will be called to question for all the good things on this earth that we did not enjoy."

And so, is there one more thing on this earth you want to try? (A good thing, please.)

If you are going through a terrible time, remember this, "This too shall pass."

I said once before, at the beginning of my book "free Feeling Real Emotions Everyday" that one of the hardest things we can do as human beings is to adapt to freedom. That's why people have committed suicide AFTER being released from concentration camps, AFTER being released from prison.

AFTER cancer, AFTER long term health problems, AFTER divorce, AFTER escaping abusive situations, AFTER...

This is why we have a thing called POST Traumatic Stress Disorder. AFTER is hard.

But we can.

We can survive the good things in life, we can adapt to freedom, we can survive the tremors that hit us, because the earthquake is done.

I believe in us, I believe in human beings, that we can grow and evolve, to be successful, to be authentic, to be who we are destined to be, we can be alive, we can feel the air on our faces, like any average dog sticking its head out of the window, on an average day and remember, "Hey, this is fun."

Hold lightly that which you cherish

All fear stems from a desire to protect ourselves (or who or what we love). When we go right down deep into it, it all stems from love, no matter the complexities of the psychology and physiology of that fear (all the logical and learned reactions and triggers we can deal with, if we work through them). Following that root down and opening our hearts, we can stay in love, in bliss and find peace and an easier way of moving towards success.

So what if the opposite of self love, the "I hate myself", the shyness and being small, quiet, the hiding, the desire to disintegrate, the self-sabotage, the negativity and even self destructive thoughts, the desire to disappear either by becoming ghost-like and unseen (almost like Paulo Coelho's becoming the wind) or even suicide, is a way of denying love, to avoid confrontation with fear? Like the film "The Day of the Dolphin" we tell ourselves we are nothing or awful or we do not love ourselves as a way of protecting ourselves.

Does it work? (Not the suicide, obviously.)

Does it help?

Could it help?

I feel that the path of the spiritual warrior is to hold two truths about ourselves and about who and what we love in the same moment. It, we, they is/are everything and nothing in the same breath.

I am the love of my own life. I am human, and also eternal, and the human part of me is everything, the part that touches the trees, the sea, that eats and sleeps and writes and has a name that will live on in my books, but this part will soon be gone. I am everything and nothing. I must hold my life as if it is the most precious and exquisite dream, and gift, I must eat my vegetables and look both ways before I cross the road, and yet, I must accept that no matter how tightly I hold on, no matter how much I strive, it could all, my personhood as described in "The Fault In Our Stars", disappear in a second.

I am everything and nothing, as is everyone and everything I love (so the world then), I am eternal and invincible and yet, like a flame, can be extinguished by a breath or a gust of wind.

So fragile, so precious, so brilliant... no wonder we are scared to embrace life, and instead make it mundane and prosaic, make ourselves small and mouse like, because the reality is heartbreaking to much of what we learn as humans. To the mindset that says things must be consistent and safe and insurable. To the ego.

Muhammad Ali, "Tomorrow is promised to no one."

Life is my Sherpa

When a climber gets to the top of Mount Everest, they don't do it alone, they do it with a Sherpa (I've written in the past about these incredible people, whose bodies actually use oxygen in a different way to most human beings, and I highly recommend you Google Lhakpa Sherpa). At a talk by an adventurer who has climbed Mount Everest, I was humbled to begin to understand the process. As he said, the adrenaline gets you to the top of the mountain, but then the adrenaline dissipates, and it's the Sherpa hitting you with a stick (only if necessary) who gets you down before you run out of oxygen and energy and you die on the mountain.

This year I felt like life was hitting me with a stick. I've called it my year of failure, but when I look back it was like every time I was tired and wanted to sit down, wanted to "just rest for a minute," life said, "No."

Nothing worked for me.

Except the very few things that were meant to.

I was less than a day away from having to sign on or ask for Universal Credit, to ask for benefits, welfare, whatever you want to call it. Something I have never done since I left university in 1993. I grew up on benefits, and we needed them, but I always said that it was my choice if I wasn't working, if I was writing or making films or running a business that wasn't really covering its costs… I am an able bodied person with two degrees and many, many skills. I have always been able to get a job when I wanted one.

My last ditch attempt to get something, to make something happen was to go to The London Book Fair in 2019. I stayed in dorm rooms at the local youth hostel for three nights, I stayed with a friend for another. She had a lovely flat, but I was sleeping on a single blow up bed and all I could think was, "I don't want to live like this." And then I got up and went to the fair and schmoozed. I spoke to recruiters, I spoke to publishers, I asked insightful questions and spoke up in panels (about subjects like accessibility and audio books), I found mentors at panels on women in leadership, I was asked to send over my CV about a dozen times, I worked it. I sent off a pitch for work that someone at the Fair switched me onto, on my laptop in the midst of things, I sent another special Fair offer to another writer who was thinking of working with me, I did everything. I smiled, I did Instagram, I did a live video with someone in the Copyright Office, I went to drinks parties and didn't get drunk. I helped people who were too drunk to get home, get home. On the last night in a party funded by Amazon (where I ate canapés for dinner to save money, my friends had fed me at the show and I'd bought end of the day food at Waitrose to heat up in the hostel), I thought to myself, wouldn't it be nice if I met a nice bloke so I wouldn't have to sleep in the youth hostel. I met a nice bloke, who was lovely and chatted and bought me drinks... and who was most perturbed to discover that I would rather go back to the hostel than to his hotel. But it was nice to have the choice.

I was homeless, I was flat broke, the Fair was over, the recruitment companies had nothing, not even warehouse work, the only work there was would have cost me more to get to than I would earn. I went to stay with family. I had done everything, I had kept the faith, I had really, really done my best. I had given my all.

On Sunday night, my first paying publishing client said yes to my London Book Fair offer and paid me my fee. It felt like a fortune. I would not have to sign on.

I was still flat broke, and a month or so later, in desperation I would email the client I didn't get at the Fair and thank goodness, she said yes that week. She paid me straight away and I could pay my bills.

And so it went on, one at a time, little by little, then a job staying with a lady with dementia, then another opportunity, one step at a time, and having to get tough on asking people to pay me for work I had done.

This little publishing company I have developed, this way of working, it is not a side hustle, or a passion project, it was and is, my way to get down off the mountain, and its success was born of desperation and quite simply seeing no other way to avoid poverty.

Many of the places I have stayed, the good work I have done, the experiences, were not adventuring, or compassion, they were survival. Doing what I would never, in other circumstances, have done.

But... this was just another part of my training (I say life may not be a rehearsal but it might just be a training – or at least, much of it) and these experiences taught me exactly what I needed to know to go on and do the impossible, be there for the people I love in new and unimagined ways, as well as to develop a great deal more humility and understanding.

Seth Godin once said, "Survival is success," meaning that just keeping a business going is a success. For me, "Success was survival," in that just getting through that time taught me, pushed me to do more and to ask for more than I ever thought I could.

Success is survival

But there is another meaning to this phrase.

As Charlie (Kelly McGillis) puts it in "Top Gun" to Maverick at the end, "You're not going to be happy unless you're going Mach 2 with your hair on fire."

If we are not doing "our thing", it doesn't feel like living. It feels like a living death.

I believe that if there ever comes a time when we cannot do the thing that defines us we will find another thing.

But if we stop doing the thing that we love, the thing that sets our heart alight, the thing that makes us feel like we're flying, out of some sort of fear, then that gift just stays inside of us, it starts to rot and stagnate and we begin to resent those who do.

It is better to try and to fail than to become an angry, bitter judge of those who are willing to go into the arena, better to be a penniless failed filmmaker than a successful self-hating critic.

I Just Can't Get It Right

I hear you.

Just remember how many of the advancements we take for granted took years, took lives to perfect. The electric light, the aeroplane, the helicopter, the heart transplant, the telephone, the internet are... no longer newsworthy. But the first time... these were headline news.

"God's delays are not God's denials."

It is hard, when we have tried for so long, but what we have to remember is that every try has taught us, changed us, and we may not understand why we have felt held back.

When they first invented the typewriter, typists typed so fast that they kept breaking the thing. So the makers changed the keyboard, they made it more difficult, so that typists would type slower and the machine wouldn't freeze.

Sometimes we need to be slowed down.

Sometimes it feels like we are stuck or delayed.

Listen to it, learn from it, like the weather that keeps us tucked up inside and stops us, unknowingly from getting into a car accident.

And there is also a moment for impatience, for saying, "No. Right here, right now."

We need just the right amount of patience.

Two Sides of the Same Coin

It was only in writing this book that finally the penny dropped (did you see what I did there) that, in fact, I have been teaching how to escape from fear of success ever since I first began my business Pearl Escapes in 2010. Only I didn't ever, ever call it this (maybe I was hiding what I was doing until it was done – until I was too far gone, out of the trap for my ego to stop me).

I said Pearl Escapes was all the good stuff. All the good stuff I had tried (check out my Guide to Healing – it's huuuuge). I said things like "Seek Your Bliss." The Zumba was just to pay the bills while I figured out what I was really doing. But every step I took with Zumba was a step out of my dark place, out of my cave and into the light. Each day I was shining a little bit brighter. I had to, to pay the mortgage. Each day I was taking another step towards success.

And then one day I figured it out. Yes, I help people escape, but what I do is "I help people feel alive". And that is different for everyone, so, in a way, explaining what I do became clearer to me, but more confusing for everyone else. And business coaches told me, you can't be for everyone, you can't do everything, and I sat there, and I said, "I do everything, for everyone". Because after all, we're all alive... we just might not feel alive.

And then I understood.

Fear of success is fear of life.

Fear of success is fear of being ourselves.

Fear of success is fear of our light.

Fear of success is fear of feeling alive.

Fear of success is fear of feeling our emotions.

Fear of success is fear of truth.

I had been fighting, escaping from fear of success for nearly ten years, but calling it another name. Chipping away at my own fear of success, learning spiritual principles, learning meditation, letting go of everything I am not, learning about love and what makes me feel alive, dancing, teaching, music, speaking, writing and publishing, travelling, swimming... but what I had been practicing over and over again was being a spiritual warrior, telling the truth, silencing the ego, acting on spirit, following my heart.

I started this book thinking I was writing something about fear of success because I couldn't find a teacher, so I'd give it a go. I am the teacher, I am my own guru, my own teacher, just as every other spiritual teacher is a fear of success teacher, a fear of life teacher, a fear of light teacher, every single book I have written has been about fear of success.

Rumpelstiltskin.

Voldemort.

Writer.

Dancer.

Speaker.

Lover.

Mother.

Whenever we bring fear to the light we discover it is false, or it is love, rooted in love, like the fears we have for ourselves and our loved ones.

The only thing we have to fear is fear itself.

The Arrogance of the Five Year Plan

I keep saying I'm being Zen, or trying to be Zen. I know what it means, sometimes. It's an extraordinary concept that we can't quite grasp, and yet the simplest of all; "Go with the flow." In some ways it's represented quite well by the words of the Dread Pirate Roberts in "The Princess Bride," "Good night, Westley. Good work. Sleep well. I'll most likely kill you in the morning."

Ray Bradbury, a rather decent writer, wrote about it in "Zen in the Art of Writing" as "Don't think about it. Do it. Then think about it." Sage words, which my younger brother already told me when I was struggling with pushing the button on publishing a bold new book.

I think it's what makes a good sailor: going where the wind blows, or using the wind wisely. Is it Zen, the advice of a good friend before he died, "Make the best plan you possibly can and then be prepared to throw it away at a moment's notice if something better comes along"?

Perhaps John Lennon called it best, "Life is what happens while you're busy making other plans."

I feel like Life is teaching me lessons right now, challenging me, pushing me, and every time I feel like I know what I'm doing, where I'm headed next, I am surprised, or more truthfully shocked. I don't like it. In the words of Julia

183

Roberts in "Pretty Woman," about planning… "I'm actually no, I'm not a planner. I wouldn't say I'm a planner. I would say I'm a kinda fly by the seat of my pants gal. You know moment to moment, yeah that's me, that's...yeah."

Somebody else once described Zen as, "Doing nothing… almost."

"Where do you want to be in five years?"

Alive probably. That would be good going.

"To be well?" Sounds like a good goal.

"For my family and friends to be well." Also important.

"To have good relationships with my family and friends."

Why don't we write these things in our five year plans? In more words from John Lennon, why are #goals not just always #happy? Perhaps because if we look closely at these goals we recognise our impermanence, and the impermanence of our friends and family - that we have only a little bit of control over these things.

We love the illusion of control, and so for me, when things shock and surprise me, what really shocks and surprises me is that I control very little. We even complain in England when the weather forecast is wrong.

A five year plan is a wonderful concept, but all I can think of is Dr Miranda Bailey in "Grey's Anatomy", "I have a right now plan." Or Tom Hanks' character in "Sleepless in Seattle," when the best plan is to just keep breathing.

It might surprise you to know, sitting here right now, that I can think of nothing better than writing a bold, broad, ambitious five year plan – because is it any less arrogant than the simplest; "I'll be alive and well, my family will all be alive and well"? That is the impossible plan, the impossible dream; I have absolutely (or almost absolutely) no control over that, the most important... the bottom line. So why shouldn't I dream all the other impossible dreams?

But, you know what, and here I would like your help, what would I dream of, as a writer, teacher, speaker, that would make me #happy? And here is another barrier to a proper five year plan – one that serves me, and not my ego. Does money buy happiness? If I had a wish fulfilment factory, what would I wish for?

-       To be an Amazon Best Seller. I did that, and it was lovely, but not fulfilling.

-       To help a good friend publish their book. I did that, and it felt great. That was fulfilling.

-       To make a living out of writing, publishing and coaching others in writing and publishing. But if I did that, I wouldn't be doing the other things for money right now that I know I'm meant to be doing.

-     To be a Sunday Times Bestseller? Would it make me happy?

-     To publish the book that I meant to write. Yes, I did that, more than once, more than nine times to be fair, and yes, if I stop, slow down and give myself a moment to look at what I've done – yes, that feat of magic brings me to tears. My books may not be perfect, but they are art.

-     To serve others. Yes, perhaps that's the biggest thing. When I have received a review or rather thank you letter from someone who I have helped.

-     To change the world? Yes, I'd like to change it slowly, I'd like to lift a mirror up and help people to see things differently. I guess I'd like the immortality of teaching something that carries on, of explaining the inexplicable, of discovering something and sharing it, the legacy of a scientist, even though my form of science is so different to what I ever expected it to be.

So, in attempting to write the future, what I have really done is to write my past, to look back, and with gratitude realise that my five year plan, so full of arrogance and expectation, is really an invitation to myself, to look back at the last five years and see where I have come from, how far I have come and to know without a doubt that I would never, ever have believed how much I could have achieved and experienced and given in the last five years if I had planned it.

I made plan after plan after plan, and I let go of each one of them when something better came along (or something worse went bump in the night,) and I went with the flow, with the wind, where it took me. And if I can just have faith that wherever the wind takes me tomorrow will also work out, then I can accept, make peace and even fall in love with my lack of control. In remembering that I may be dead by morning, I can embrace and fall in love with this day, this beautiful day, whether it rains or storms or snows, and when I am downhearted by thinking of what I need, or what I think I need, or where I've failed or fallen, I can remember that just as "Nothing is Permanent," "Anything is Possible."

The Sum of Fears

"You may take the most gallant sailor, the most intrepid airman, or the most audacious soldier, put them at a table together—what do you get? The sum of their fears." Winston Churchill, 16 November 1943

Sometimes we have to work alone. Our fear alone is enough to handle. It is enough to heal ourselves, or to take ourselves away from the masses to avoid infecting others, because yes, fear is contagious.

I have brought these fears of success together, not to increase them, but so that you can see them more clearly, so you can hold up your own fear to the light and see it fade.

Our fear of success, your fear of success may well be a combination of these, or perhaps the origin of your fear of success is something different, as different as the airman's from the sailor's. That's okay. In fact, it may be better that way, by looking at my fears, which are not your own, you may be able to see them more clearly than I can, and then, when you turn back to your own, you may be able to see your own more clearly too.

The only way out is through.

We have to combat our own fears, our own prejudices so that we do not pass them on to the next generation. As hard as we may want to protect them, in protecting them too much we do them a disservice.

We may need to teach them not to talk to strangers or wander off, but one day those skills may be their greatest assets.

My wandering off and talking to strangers is the only way for me to come home.

The Helicopter Story

There's a story I tell often, and often to "spiritual people" – when we're discussing things like manifesting and finding our paths. I believe everything happens for a reason, but sometimes it might not be your reason and you can drive yourself nuts thinking about, "Why me? Why this?"

All I know is that if I forget about it and get on with my life, very often those things come around and I realise why I needed those experiences. Very often things happen to help us learn lessons, or to point us in the right direction, or to test us or the people around us. Perhaps they are all moments of truth.

The problem with popular ways of thinking about manifesting is that they give people a lazy or God-complex attitude. I wanted a million dollars and so I manifested a million dollars. I kept saying I want a brown Ford and I got a brown Ford.

My take on this – it's a lot like Chandler in the first episode of "Friends". Ross says, "I just want to be married again," and in walks Rachel in a wet wedding dress. So Chandler turns and says, "And I just want a million dollars."

I don't want to tell you how to think about the universe or religion, it's important that you think for yourself. In fact, at a certain point all great teachers will tell you, "Don't believe anything," you have to find your own truth – you have to

191

wander in the wilderness for yourself. You can only learn so much in a sex education class, at some point you have to go off and do it (or dance, if that analogy is a bit hot for you).

"Ask and it shall be given." But for me, the best way of describing the universe is as the wisest, most generous teacher. And if I ask for a million pounds (and believe me, there have been moments), or a hot boyfriend, or huge critical success, it's not going to happen. Because the universe is still busy delivering on the bigger things I asked for, things like understanding the nature of life, of love, things I asked for in my best moments, like when I sat in a Kona wind in Hawai'i and asked to serve the world because I had achieved what I always wanted, an understanding of unconditional love.

This great and perfect teacher is not just going to give me an "A," because it knows that I want to do the work, I want to serve, I want to make the cake from scratch.

Going back to the "Friends" analogy, what was really going on? (I know, it's fictional, but let's play with it.) I would say that Ross is in tune with the universe with his timing, with his desire, the feeling of wanting to go back, although, of course, his feeling is nothing new – it's been months, right?

Rachel is also in tune, and desperate. In a moment of truth she jumped out of the window and out of her life, and "luckily" she had let her friendship with Monica slide, so there was someone she could go to.

We know, from all the other series, that Ross and Rachel are connected, maybe destined to be together, so for me, in this moment, this need on both sides pulls them together. Rachel needs someone to tell her and show her that there is life outside of marriage. Ross needs someone to tell him and show him that there is life after marriage.

Ross did not manifest Rachel. Rachel did not manifest Monica or Ross.

But an ego driven understanding of how the universe works says, "Hey, I just thought about it, and focused on it and it showed up."

And Chandler says, "And I just want a million dollars."

So what's the helicopter story?

A man of God (any religion or practice will do) gets caught with a load of people he is trying to help, in a terrible flood.

They shelter on top of a building, and he starts to pray, "Please God, help us."

Pretty soon a rowboat comes along. They help all the people into the boat and then the skipper says, "Come on, get in."

"No, no, you go ahead and save the rest of the poor

stranded people. God will save me."

They shake their heads, but they have to get everyone to the hospital so off they go.

And he sits, and it's pretty cold up there, and he says, "Please God, save all the people stranded. Please help me to be brave."

Pretty soon a speedboat comes along, and they say, "Jump in, we'll get you to the hospital."

"No, no, you must help all the other stranded people. God will save me."

They shrug and keep going.

All of a second he hears a noise and above him is a helicopter. They drop down a rope, but he shakes his head, and shouts up to them, "Save the others first."

Night falls. It gets really cold, and dark, and he feels his life ebbing away.

He finds himself standing in heaven. God in all his (or her) glory sits before him.

The man shakes his head, "I don't understand."

God looks at him sadly.

"I've been a deeply religious man my whole life, I've served you wisely, I've helped hundred, thousands of people in need, I've set up schools, I've nursed the sick, why, when I needed you most, did you desert me, did you leave me to die alone on a rooftop in a flood?"

194

God shakes his (or her) head again and says, "Well I don't understand either... I sent you a rowboat, I sent you a speedboat, I sent you a helicopter..."

This book is for you and it is for me. It may be more of a rowboat than a helicopter, you have to get in and do some work. And I, I need to work these practices and ideas too, but this book is intended as a lifesaver. (Like a red ring hanging by a canal, like a fire extinguisher, like the red box around something with the words "Break glass in case of emergency".)

The first time I tried to read "The Road Less Travelled" I could not. There were some ideas in there I could not handle. A few years later, having beaten down some of the origins of my own hang ups I was ready. I didn't agree with it all, but I could read it and say, "Yes, this bit is useful", "No, I don't buy this bit."

When I have a massage the most important work is usually on the sorest spots. But sometimes I can't even take that, I have to ask them to go easy on me, because this work we are doing together, you and I, and the world, is healing, and it can be painful and messy, and expensive and it is work. And you are brave (or maybe desperate) to pick this book up in the first place. You have chosen to confront the deepest fear of the human race.

Well done.

And I know exactly what you are going to get out of this work if you continue. I don't know how hard this will be for you, whether you will master fear of success in a moment, or if it will take you years, I don't know if you will keep going, give up, or decide to take another path, work with another coach, but I know what the reward is.

You will have adventures, you will experience excitement, and the unhealed parts of you will come to the fore to be treated, you will have fun.

You will, as Joey in "Friends" put it to Ross on life after marriage (using the analogy of dating as being in an ice cream parlour), "Grab a spoon."

Do not be afraid of your reward, do not be afraid of the magnificence you feel within you, do not be afraid of happy endings and winning the lottery, do not be afraid of things going right, do not be afraid of catching up to your dreams, do not be afraid of painting with every colour in your palette, using all the many gifts that you got given, do not be afraid of heights, of altitude sickness, do not be afraid of the darkness, do not be afraid of the light, do not be afraid of yourself. You are a miracle.

Your reward is the greatest gift of all, it is life.

THE END

About the Author

I'm Pearl. When I came up with the concept of Pearl Escapes, as well as the escape in a box, my goal was to share all of the wonderful things I was discovering, especially spas, with everyone around the world. At the time I gave myself the tongue in cheek title of Explorer-in-Chief, and it stuck.

Over the nine years since then, I realised that I was really sharing healing, I've tried over 500 types, and my 2019 book on healing is, I believe, the most complete guide to forms of healing in the world. Ultimately what I do is simply to help people feel alive and, although this path challenges me at times, I have the greatest reward for doing this; whenever I get lost and stop following the beat of my own drum – whenever I start trying to be someone that I'm not, the universe puts me, one way or another, back on my path and makes me feel alive again.

Please do check out all the books I've written as I really hope, especially in the healing guide, that there is something there for every single person around the world who is hurting, healing or just comfortably numb. I have learned, over the last nine years, that whether we walk alone or dance at a convention, we heal together, because as any spiritual guru worth their salt will tell you – we are all connected.

Buen camino!

\|/

For more check out www.pearlescapes.co.uk or follow me on Instagram @pearlescapes (I am on Facebook, Twitter and LinkedIn but Instagram is home).

Oh and don't forget I'm a real person and you can email me, pearl@pearlescapes.co.uk - I love hearing your stories too.

Acknowledgements

Thank you for buying and reading this book, I made it just for you.

And thank you to all the many people, places and animals who have helped me on my journey – thank you for taking care of me, thank you for loving me.

\|/

There is always a moment for me, when things have become impossible, when I seek for a way forward and somehow find an answer, when things seem to fit into place, but I am still jangling from the impossible moments, and so I meditate, I silence my mind and listen to the universe, and in that moment it is hard to hear the universe because all I can hear is my soul loudly roaring, "Thank you for my life."

Also by the Author

All Empires Fall (financial thriller)

Camino de la Luna Series (self-help/travel) - available with photos as full colour paperbacks and colour pdf eBooks. The first few audiobooks are out now

Japan Is Very Wonderful

free Feeling Real Emotions Everyday

Camino de la Luna – Take What You Need

Camino de la Luna – Unconditional Love

Camino de la Luna – Forgiveness

Camino de la Luna – Compassion and Self Compassion

Camino de la Luna – Courage

Camino de la Luna – Truth

Camino de la Luna – Reconciliation

Pearl Escapes Guide to Healing 2019 - Massage, Meditation, Spa Treatments, Teachers, Practices and Places (Seventh Edition)

The Guide to Spa Breaks and Escapes from Pearl Escapes (various editions)

Meditation for Angry People

The Wee, The Wound And The Worries: My Experience Of Being A Kidney Donor

Pearl Escapes Mini-Guides (various locations)

Love And The Perfect Wave (romantic novel)

Printed in Great Britain
by Amazon

30111657R00112